Playing the Strategy Game

Playing the Strategy Game

Strategy is a skill not a formula.

Make it one of yours.

PATRICK THURBIN

FINANCIAL TIMES

Prentice Hall

an imprint of Pearson Education

London • New York • San Francisco • Toronto • Sydney • Tokyo • Singapore • Hong Kong

Cape Town • Madrid • Paris • Milan • Munich • Amsterdam

PEARSON EDUCATION LIMITED

Head Office:
Edinburgh Gate
Harlow CM20 2JE
Tel: +44 (0)1279 623623
Fax: +44 (0)1279 431059

London Office:
128 Long Acre
London WC2E 9AN
Tel: +44 (0)20 7447 2000
Tel: +44 (0)20 7240 5771
Website: www.business-minds.com

First published in Great Britain in 2001

© Pearson Education Limited 2001

The right of Patrick J. Thurbin to be identified as Author of this Work has been asserted
by him in accordance with the Copyright, Designs and Patents Act 1988.

ISBN 0 273 65424 1

British Library Cataloguing in Publication Data
A CIP catalogue record for this book can be obtained from the British Library

10 9 8 7 6 5 4 3 2 1

Designed by Claire Brodmann Book Designs, Lichfield, Staffs.
Typeset by Northern Phototypesetting Co. Ltd, Bolton
Printed and bound in Great Britain by Biddles Ltd, Guildford & King's Lynn

The Publishers' policy is to use paper manufactured from sustainable forests.

About the author

Patrick J. Thurbin is Principal Business Consultant and Strategy Lecturer at the Business School, Kingston University in the UK. He combines a wide range of consulting assignments in national and multinational organizations with research and lecturing at the University. His activities provide an exposure to leading business thinking and practices in many cultures, industries and organizations. He is a Director of the well-established Open Learning MBA program at the University, leading the team that teaches business strategy; he has lectured as a Visiting Professor in Management at Grand Valley State University in Michigan, USA; and in business strategy at the prestigious Academy of National Economy in Moscow, Russia.

Patrick's research on ways in which business growth can be supported by leveraging organizational knowledge is extensive. His book *Leveraging Knowledge* (FT Prentice Hall) provides an international benchmark in this area. A determination to promote a critical approach in the strategic thinking used by managers resulted in the publication of the ground breaking text *The Influential Strategist* (FT Pitman, 1998). This championed the use of key organizational paradoxes to diagnose and harness the tensions within organizations that create winning stretagies. His consulting activities range over industries as diverse as aerospace, retail and distribution, software development and civil engineering, where innovative approaches to business growth is the main focus.

Before becoming an academic and author, Patrick spent some 20 years working in the UK, Europe and the USA, gaining practical management and business experience in design, production, research and information systems development.

This book is dedicated to
Daisy, my Georgia Girl.

Contents

Acknowledgements   *page* xi
Preface   xiii
Introduction   xix

Part 1 Understanding the strategy game   1

1 Business as a competitive game   3
Identifying what drives your performance   3
Case study: Caterer seeks recipe for tasty growth   3
The rules of the game   11
Who are the key players and what makes them so?   15

2 Some fundamental beliefs about business success   19
What can the gurus tell us?   19
Henry Mintzberg's ten schools of thought   21
What can successful companies tell us?   28
Case study: Walt Disney   28
Case study: Compaq   30
Case study: Nokia   31
Summary   32

Part 2 Becoming a better strategist   35

3 The quest for a business logic   37
Identifying your business approach   37
Case study: Recipes for a healthier brand image   37
Finding the best approach   44
Case study: GEC   46
Is it all about having a superior business model?   48
The McGahan study   49
What does this research tell us?   55
The fixed plan v. flexibility paradox   57
Case study: Netscape   57

4 The reality of business strategy 59
Believing in a winning idea 59
Why we believe in a winning business logic 61
Case study: Ford Motor Company 62
Case study: The Body Shop 63
Three generic strategies 64
Case study: American Express 66
Applying the generic strategies 68
For a business, the past becomes the present 72

5 Why is everyone reinventing the wheel? 75
For houses the word is "location"; for business it's "context" 75
Putting contemporary business thinking in context 77
Has www.com made your business thinking obsolete? 79
Organizational entrepreneurship 81
Summary 83

Part 3 Generic skills behind effective strategic behavior 85

Introduction 87

A. Integrating personal and business development agendas 89

6 Developing personal strategies 91
Emotional and fundamental beliefs 91
Maintaining the vision 95
Setting personal goals 96
Personality and cognitive style 100
Summary 107

7 Developing business strategies 109
Matching strategic thinking to the business context 109
Linking development to implementation 117
Valuing and learning from experience 123
Summary 127

B. Winning support for your strategies 129

8 Influencing others 131
Using mental maps 131

Handling power and politics 135
Handling the culture and your impact on others 143
Tapping into your natural leadership 148
Gaining recognition 156
Summary 159

9 Taking action in context 163
Balancing the stakeholders 163
Is it sensible to try to control performance? 169
Summary 176

C. Developing your strategic sense and imagination 179

10 Learning how to adapt 181
Harnessing your creativity 181
Accelerating your learning 190
Confront basic assumptions 195
Summary 196

11 Intuition, the ultimate skill 197
Developing vision 197
Being a visionary 201
Using your imagination 202
Develop your intuition 206
Summary 208

Epilogue 211
Index 215

Acknowledgements

I am indebted to the many CEOs whose efforts in developing and growing businesses make it possible to write such books. Also to Pradeep Jethi and Richard Stagg who provided the professional back up that underpinned the writing process. Acknowledgement is also due to the publishing team at Pearson Education, in particular Fiona Ramsay and Linda Dhondy for editing the original manuscript and managing the project.

A book such as this must also acknowledge the many writers whose thoughts have influenced my thinking. Many of them are already famous and it would be pretentious to mention them here. But my particular acknowledgements would go to: Kees Van der Heijden for his work on the "business idea"; Richard Whittington for his contribution to the understanding of strategic thinking; and Mehrad Baghai, Stephen Coley and David White, from McKinsey and Company Inc., for sharing the hard-earned practical wisdom contained in their book, *The Alchemy of Growth*.

On a more personal level I would like to acknowledge the insight gained from knowing and talking with Bob Engle. A true American and a role model for all business entrepreneurs, Bob opened my eyes to what really counts in business. Also particular thanks to Dean Samouel and all my colleagues at Kingston Business School who continue to act as a source of inspiration and support in my work.

Preface

The current business climate is one of hyper competition, between companies and individuals. This puts immense pressures on managers. Success comes to those who become skilled at effective strategic thinking and behavior. The imperative is to understand and become a true player in this competitive game.

This book provides a breakthrough for the reader who wants to harness these pressures and acquire the skills that will create the complete strategist. The book enables readers to:

– analyze their approach to business development and compare it to that used by the top league players

– analyze and update their personal skills base

– discover how to apply these skills and link their personal agenda to that of the organization or corporate body

– become key players in the modern competitive business game.

It will help you to develop your strategic thinking and act as a coach to help you adopt effective strategic behaviors.

Every manager is involved either directly or indirectly in helping to develop the organization's business. How best to do this is a question that is faced every day and at every hour. We are told that to succeed in the business world it is important to have a good grasp or understanding of how organizations compete and what causes some to win and others to lose. An understanding that the professional manager acquires from a mixture of experience, native cunning and a study of contemporary thinking and business theory. Then we are encouraged to pick the best from all of this and tailor our approach to the challenge being faced. This is sound advice but our approaches to competing vary enormously and they are very personal. We each have to seek continually for a balance between the pressures that come from the business setting, our personal agendas and strategic behavior. What we really need is an overarching strategy for ourselves. A strategy that addresses all three. We need to get personal with strategy.

We need help to establish what I describe as a set of generic skills that will enable us to develop and apply this overarching and very personal strategy. I will provide guidance and support through all of the necessary steps to creating that strategy and point out where safe short cuts can be taken. You now have a guide and mentor for a journey of discovery that will enable you to link your personal agenda to that of the corporation.

Common sense tells us that developing a successful business requires a mixture of good luck and the insight of one or more key players. Business is driven by individuals, and at times by individuals working together. Many of us have ambitions to emulate the successes of media heroes such as George Soros, Marjorie Scardino, Richard Branson, Bill Gates, Ted Turner, Rupert Murdoch, Anita Roddick. You probably have your own heroes. If you are anything like me you probably attribute their success to having amazing insight, a penchant for hard work, a foundation of rich experiences and a good dose of luck. In our more cynical moments we probably complain that they were just fortunate to get a good start in life and be in the right place at the right time. But we know that it is, of course, more than luck, they are all good at playing the strategy game. One thing that top strategists share is an ability to convert experiences and knowledge into a personalized skills base that sustains all their efforts. Their thinking and action appears, to us, to be natural. There is a smooth flow from recognition of a complex set of circumstances to decision making and action. You and I quickly recognize such mastery and would like to have the knowledge and skills on which it is based. One way that we can do this is by putting ourselves in situations that force us to experiment and learn. If we are lucky then we will survive long enough to reach the point where our talents are recognized. I am offering you a way of avoiding a life sentence that involves a perpetual search for success and having to depend on good luck.

You may well have pondered over why it is that, with all the effort that has been put into theorizing and writing about business and personal development, the way to success is still not clear. Even those that are fortunate enough to find a pathway appear to be constrained by the very skills and knowledge that they have so painstakingly acquired. Now is the time to break this pattern. I will provide the opportunity for you to find your way through the maze of learning opportunities. Together we will pick out and expose the many myths that have been created by those purporting

I am offering you a way of avoiding a life sentence that involves a perpetual search for success and having to depend on good luck

to have found the winning approach. Then I will help you to acquire the generic skills and understanding that can be used to create your personal strategic agenda and link it to that of the organization.

What do I mean by a generic skills base? We talk about skills around everyday issues such as driving, playing golf and social behavior. As the range of situations in which our skills are applied increases they become more ingrained. We reach a point where we are recognized by our skills and the approaches that we regularly use to manage our work and our lives. They become part of our persona. We can change our approaches but this usually only happens when a catastrophic event occurs or when we see a high pay-off. Our learned approaches represent a complex combination of knowledge, developed skills, experience and, most importantly, our personal motivation. It is this combination that sets us out among a crowd.

As a manager you will have already developed approaches that you rely on to deal with operational and the more strategic issues. For most managers there is now a much closer time or thinking gap between operations and strategy. In many industries differentiating between the two has become a luxury. You are likely to have undertaken formal management studies and attended company based and professional courses. Exposure to the press and the media will have kept you up to date with the latest thinking in business and personal development. You have become a professional manager. But what is missing is a clear way for you to check out whether those ingrained approaches that are part of your armament, are helping or hindering performance. You also need a way of checking whether your approaches are effective in the different contexts in which you work. For example, when faced with a strategic issue, here I mean one that has a longer-term implication, you probably like to be clear about the objectives that have to be met, who the key stakeholders are and what they expect from you. This may be an appropriate approach, but in some cases it can result in serious flaws in your performance. For example, in a chaotic

> Armed with the generic skills and understanding that are revealed in this book, you will then be able to get personal with strategy

and fast-moving context, thinking about objectives or even believing that outcomes can be determined could be a fatal mistake. At this point you are probably thinking that I am stating the obvious, but it is vital that we recognize, and agree, that many of your approaches are heavily ingrained. Unlearning is easier said than done. By reading this book you will expose approaches that have become part of your psyche. I can then show you how to mold these into a formula for personal success giving you a whole new approach to linking your corporate and personal strategic agendas. Armed with the generic skills and understanding that are revealed in this book, you will then be able to get personal with strategy.

Business and personal development involves making sense of complexity and uncertainty. We do this by forming mental models that help us to explain how things work. Unfortunately, application of some conventional frameworks favored by management consultants, academics and the gurus, have relied on explanation rather than understanding. No doubt many executives have adopted these simple models and used them to drive their organizations to the brink of disaster before someone managed to recognize what was happening and tried to apply the brakes. Downsizing, empowerment and a host of others have all had their devotees and extracted their toll on businesses. Henry Ford's offer to give every customer the option of having a car of any color as long as it was black has become an apocryphal story. The game play was valid until the context for which it had been designed changed dramatically. General Motors seized the advantage by introducing a game play based on differentiation and choice. So there is an obvious danger in using business formulae that do not fit the context. Particularly one that is not shared by the people we count on for support.

The first thing that the book provides is an opportunity for you to analyze your approach to managing and developing a highly competitive business, developing the idea of business as a game played between players who use different rules and have different personal agendas. We round off this early section with a review of some fundamental beliefs about how to make a success of developing and growing a business. This provides a vital summary and critique of the tools of strategic thinking and business development. It is essential that we tackle this in a rigorous way. The danger of not doing this is that we might be tempted to set out on our quest carrying a lot of surplus baggage. Those cherished beliefs such as market positioning and building on core competences might prove to be the basis of some dangerous approaches that have become ingrained. Other basic concepts might have been misunderstood, or missed completely, and have created an imbalance in the way that you deal with the complexity that surrounds business development. But in tackling business and personal development we must avoid the temptation of working in isolation.

Whether we like to admit it or not, we all rely on others. Each day we interact with our managers and colleagues, relying on a set of hard earned approaches to make life manageable. These approaches are influenced and given life by those we work with and through. But we often find ourselves faced with challenges to our preferred approach. For example, we may have a very clear way of dealing with an investment decision, an approach to a joint venture or stimulating innovation at a product level. But these approaches become futile unless they are recognized and shared by our colleagues. Here we see one of the generic skills. The skill used when we are trying to discover how our colleagues are making sense of a complex issue. Their understanding will be driven by the three pressures that we are ourselves seeking to balance.

Those created by the business context or setting, our personal agendas and strategic behaviors. What we have to discover is how our ingrained approaches help or hinder our ability to work with others. But we also need to recognize the importance of context.

How we interpret the setting or context in which the organization operates becomes a major determinant of our actions. We need to ensure that our way of doing this is based on an approach which proves effective and has a reality that can be shared with colleagues. Attempts to analyze the business context will immediately bring us up against a host of techniques and advice from the ubiquitous PEST and the familiar Porters 5 Forces, to the more stretching notions of scenario planning. But the very fact that we are contemplating such a prescriptive set of frameworks could be an indicator of an ingrained approach that needs revising.

> What we have to discover is how our ingrained approaches help or hinder our ability to work with others. But we also need to recognize the importance of context

If all that it took to create a winning business was a set of easily learned skills, then there would be fewer businesses. The winning firms would by now have attracted the best strategists in the land and have encapsulated the rules for profit, individual well-being and harmony in tablets of stone. We know that this is not the case. My contention is that the opportunity for success, both in business and in life, depends on acquiring and using a set of generic skills. But that these skills, once acquired, soon become translated and ingrained as personalized approaches. Because we all have different agendas, both personal and corporate, application of these skills and our ingrained approaches will result in different outcomes. It is the variety of approaches that creates the diversity of management and of performance among firms and individuals. If this is the case then creating a close link between how we make sense of business complexity and our personal strategic agendas must be a quest worth pursuing. Unless we do this then we really are going to have to wait for someone else to impose their ambitions on our destiny and our chances of success. Why wait to be handed a good strategy when you can become a good strategist? For many managers this is a decision that they will have already made. But here I am offering you the chance to break out of the trap that management education, the advice of the gurus and your own experiences have created. A chance to acquire a set of generic skills and developed approaches that will survive changes to contemporary beliefs about best business practice and personal development and the impact of an increasingly turbulent business environment.

This book presents a "once and for all" approach to obtaining mastery over the fundamentals of strategic thinking and hence the pressures that are presented in this modern world in which we live and work. It is aimed at the informed, ambitious but critical reader. Many tried and trusted beliefs about how to manage business and personal development will be challenged. I have deliberately created a boundary breaking book in order to help you to succeed and to promote a new wave of thinking and action among key management players. I invite you to begin this quest for success.

Introduction

As a business manager you cannot wait to be handed a good strategy and personal growth is too important to leave to chance. I have written this book to help you take ownership of your own strategic thinking and to coach you in developing effective strategic behaviors. Winning the strategy game is a skill and, contrary to popular belief, much less a process that can be learned and then followed.

The challenge is to master the fundamentals of strategic thinking and become a better player of the strategy game. With the right skills base it is possible to rise above simply settling for business and personal survival or at worst opting out. You need to discover how strategy works for you and take ownership of your imagination. It is time to remove those inhibitions that are constraining your true potential. With this book you can create your own strategies and not have to live someone else's.

The challenge is to master the fundamentals of strategic thinking and become a better player of the strategy game

To develop that unique and personal strategy you will need to:

- understand the rules and formulae that businesses use to play the strategy game
- understand how you approach and play the business development game
- learn how to create the right strategies for you and your business
- acquire the key skills needed to integrate personal and corporate strategic agendas.

Helping you to develop a strategy that links your personal and business goals has been my motivation for writing this book. Acquiring a set of personal skills will set you on the path to becoming the complete strategist. Going beyond how to think. Tackling how to *be*.

The suggestion that we make sense of complex issues and take action using a personal skills base is not earth shattering. We all develop unique approaches that guide or at times dominate our actions and thoughts. They are the means by which we appear to ourselves and our colleagues to be able to make sense of and handle complexity in life and business situations. Confidence and success are usually attributed to someone having discovered a set of winning approaches, be they a tennis champion or a top business executive. If we are going to acquire new approaches or change those that we have, then we need to look at their source. They are derived from:

- experiences gained from working in a number of contexts
- internalized knowledge
- applying knowledge
- personal and often secret goals
- personal motivation that is driven by contextual pressures
- emotional and fundamental beliefs
- what you know, and are prepared to admit, about the impact of your behavior on others.

These are all powerful drivers that influence us at a subconscious level. We are in many ways victims of these drivers. Hence my line of attack is to remove the clutter and noise that surrounds this base on which your approaches have been built. But our approaches are only revealed when we see the impact of their application. They become real and observable only through action. My book forces you to confront this reality by presenting you with actual business situations that give a clear view of:

- your current approach to managing yourself
- how your current approaches impact on your efforts to develop the business
- how your approaches need to be developed and molded so that you can create a link between personal and organizational agendas.

I have provided a series of reviews throughout the book to help you achieve this breakthrough in insight and thinking.

My job is to help you to discover how best to achieve this breakthrough in the context of your own organization. To do this I have isolated the set of generic skills that you need to acquire and learn to apply in context. You will already be capable, along with thousands of others, of carrying out the tasks and functional activities involved in developing a busi-

Successful individuals have an intuitive appreciation of how to apply knowledge and skills in different contexts

ness and handling operational situations. But what you will have discovered is that successful individuals have an intuitive appreciation of how to apply knowledge and skills in different contexts. Ingrained approaches enable them to tackle complex issues with practiced familiarity and apparent panache. They are able to make sense of complexity.

This book gives you an opportunity to review the basis on which your approaches have been built. I will then help you to add to this knowledge base and develop an overarching strategy that bridges your personal and the corporate agendas. We are going beyond the conventional theories and drilling down to a personal level. The skills that you will acquire include:

- developing personal strategies
- developing business strategies
- influencing others
- taking action in context
- learning how to adapt
- harnessing your intuition.

As with any breakthrough in thinking, the new approach appears simple. Watson and Crick, in solving the riddle of the double helix of the DNA chain, for which they were awarded the Nobel Prize, are alleged to have been embarrassed that the solution could be written on one page. If we asked the average manager, trainer or management guru what they thought about our quest to acquire the skills listed above, they would argue that they are, at first glance, well documented and readily achieved. But a moment's reflection will show that although these are generic, their power can only be released when they are practiced and honed on a test bed of active business management. We all know how to run, but becoming a world beater requires that we acquire a set of generic skills and learn to apply them as part of a process of mastering ourselves and our environment. After many years, and with enough good fortune, you will, no doubt, have faced all the situations that are essential to developing these generic skills. Some skills will have become ingrained, and in spite of evidence that they do not apply in all situations, you are probably reluctant to give them up. This book gives you the opportunity to take time out and check the skills that you have acquired and for the less experienced manager, you have an opportunity to accelerate along the learning curve.

There are hundreds of books that tell us about business and personal development. Thousands of examples of what has been attempted and what has transpired in a host of contexts. It is not unreasonable for you to wonder why it is that major errors are made by some of the best informed, educated, experienced and powerful managers in the world. My contention is that every manager uses a range of well developed approaches. They do not simply apply the knowledge and advice contained in the latest fashionable management books. They graft any new knowledge on to ingrained approaches that have been acquired from experience and studies, in a range of contexts. These ingrained approaches drive their interpretation of the business and social contexts, how they evaluate the various options and make decisions. What differentiates the outcomes of all this brilliant effort, is the variety between the approaches that the individual is using, and our old friend: luck. My point is that it is your approach that will determine your success or failure in both business and life. Acquiring the skills described in this book will enable you to break through the mystery that surrounds the search for a set of winning approaches that will establish your personal strategy and strategic behaviors.

It is your approach that will determine your success or failure in both business and life

The way forward is therefore clear. I will help you to uncover the truths and challenge the myths surrounding contemporary and leading edge business thinking, making certain that you have taken on board the knowledge and understanding that is required. Ensuring that you are aware of the hidden biases that your personality and style are creating. We will then need to check out your understanding of the generic skills and make certain that you are confident to undertake any reshaping or further developments that are required. You will have begun your journey of exploration, the rest is action.

A guide to the book:

The structure of the book acknowledges that, as a busy manager, you are looking for either new insights or for deeper understanding of issues that are impacting on your current performance. I have also taken into account that you will be experienced and already know a great deal about the business functions, operational activities and business development. You are by no means an empty cup waiting to be filled. Your exposure to the messy and personal confrontations involved in both business and life will have tempered your enthusiasm with a touch of cynicism. Using the vernacular, you are, by now, "streetwise." My main assumption, which guided my structuring of this book, is that you will be critical. I expect and want you to be constantly comparing the ideas in the book with your view of the business world. It is possible to use the book as a reference and guide to the intricacies and subtleties of business and personal development. But the true benefit is in using it to develop the personal strength and capability needed to become the complete strategist.

The book is presented in three parts:

1. Understanding the strategy game
2. Becoming a better strategist
3. The generic skills behind effective strategic behavior.

Figure I.1 shows how the book is focused on creating a link between your personal and corporate strategic agendas. The emphasis is on achieving superior performance in the business game. This is dependent on your acquiring the skills base on which business and personal development can be built. This skills base then drives how you approach and make sense of your working context and handle the perceived pressures. The book accepts that much of your personal development will stem from your efforts to succeed in the workplace. It is therefore essential to start the book with a thorough review of what

Figure I.1   **Key elements of the book**

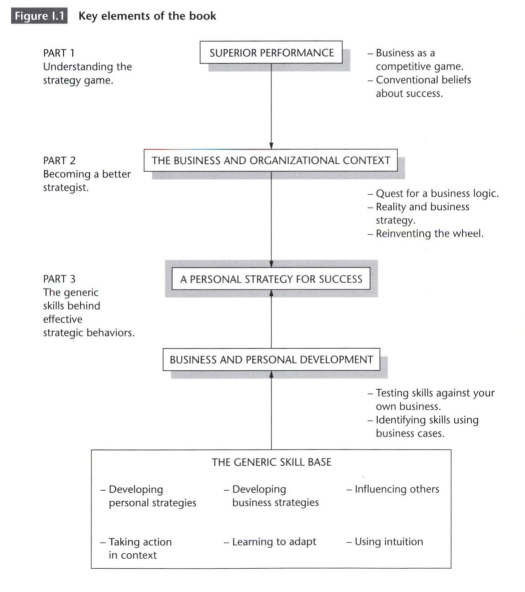

PART 1
Understanding the
strategy game.

SUPERIOR PERFORMANCE

– Business as a
  competitive game.
– Conventional beliefs
  about success.

PART 2
Becoming a better
strategist.

THE BUSINESS AND ORGANIZATIONAL CONTEXT

– Quest for a business logic.
– Reality and business
  strategy.
– Reinventing the wheel.

PART 3
The generic
skills behind
effective
strategic behaviors.

A PERSONAL STRATEGY FOR SUCCESS

BUSINESS AND PERSONAL DEVELOPMENT

– Testing skills against your
  own business.
– Identifying skills using
  business cases.

THE GENERIC SKILL BASE

– Developing
  personal strategies

– Developing
  business strategies

– Influencing others

– Taking action
  in context

– Learning to adapt

– Using intuition

drives your performance in business and to expose some of the rules of the competitive business game. Then to analyze your approach to developing a business and where this needs to be refocused. Finally the book helps you analyze the skills base that you are using and tests your thinking and ingrained approaches using some case examples and your own business situation.

Part 1, **Understanding the strategy game**, assumes that you have read a lot about business development and gained some hard-earned experience. It provides an introduction to the ideas in the book and shows how your approach to making sense of complexity, is based on knowledge, experience and personal motivation. By way of introduction you will be given a tour of the way in which strategic management has become a cornerstone of business thinking. Some of the core beliefs of practicing managers are reviewed alongside the characteristic behaviors of the modern business strategist.

Part 2, **Becoming a better strategist**, presents a direct assault on contemporary strategic management thinking and the way that it suggests that there are a set of recipes and rules that, if followed, will lead to success. I will help you to confront some of the chestnuts that can be found in MBA or executive management programs and in the consultant's medicine bag. The purpose of this section is to strip away some of the noise that surrounds business management theory and practice. Improving your ability to play the competitive business game may involve some nasty shocks. Some ingrained beliefs that have been built on old models and theories have to be challenged. To do this I will present current thinking about what constitutes best practice business development in a way that will help you to decide what to keep and what to jettison. The section also provides a basic approach to making sense of complexity as a way of testing out how robust these contemporary beliefs really are. We can then move on to Part 3.

Part 3, **Generic skills behind effective strategic behavior**, becomes the engine of the book and also the pay-off. You will be presented with an opportunity to analyze your skills and then shown how they can be practiced and applied. The section begins by establishing the personal and work-based foundations of the skills that you need to master. Showing you how to master yourself and helping you to review your goals, personality and cognitive style. You are then given detailed guidance on how to recognize anomalies that occur throughout the business development process and how these can be managed. The next step is to look at the skills involved in influencing others, using the organizational culture, handling the politics and the pressures in your work context. The importance of providing clear messages and leading from the front is linked to ways of gaining support from the power group to support action taking. The final skills areas are those of learning to adapt to the changing work scene and using your intuition. Here I will focus on how you can accelerate your learning and keep up to date with the latest thinking. You will also be shown how to acquire and use insight. I will provide you with a guide on how to link your personal strategic agenda to that of the organization. Figure I.2 below shows the skills that you will need to acquire in your quest to develop a winning personal strategy.

In summary this book will help you to:

- understand strategic thinking and the strategic management process
- create better strategies more quickly
- create the right strategies for you and your business
- communicate and win support for your strategies
- develop your own strategic sense and imagination
- link your corporate and personal agendas.

You will find this book both interesting and rewarding. I have set out to help you challenge old notions that have separated personal development strategies from those that focus on developing a business. In my enthusiasm to help you to learn how to integrate the two it is vital that I clear the fog and confront the myths that surround these areas. There are some excellent examples of contemporary best practice but new ideas have to be found and enshrined. The effective strategist is the manager who can see clearly what is to be believed and what is to be used. By harnessing best practice in business development to a set of generic but personalized set of skills you will have made strategy personal. This is a ground breaking book in that I am relating to you as someone with experience and knowledge. By adopting a structured approach to thinking about the foundation of your hard-earned management approaches and how they link to action, we will have accomplished a breakthrough in thinking and action.

Figure I.2 **The generic skills base**

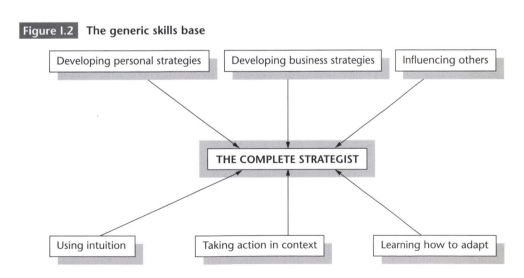

Part **1**

Understanding
the strategy game

1

Business as a competitive game

> Man is a gaming animal. He must always be trying
> to get the better in something or other
>
> *Charles Lamb (1775–1843) British Essayist*

Identifying what drives your performance

This book is about how to use a set of unique skills to achieve personal and business success. A good place to start is to check out how you would approach a complex business situation. I have provided you with a typical business scenario and your challenge is to read it, then answer some questions. Allow about 15 minutes for the reading, then 5 minutes to answer the questions. I am asking you to respond quickly because I am trying to bring out the ingrained habits that you use to make sense of the situation.

Caterer seeks recipe for tasty growth

Andrew Nelson is the last of a vanishing breed. In a rapidly consolidating industry, he stands out. But the admirable Nelson is now facing a battle to avoid being trapped in no man's land between giant corporations and ultra-small, specialist players.

Nelson Hind, the company of which he is founder managing director, has built its business offering a bespoke contract catering service through a highly decentralized power structure. But in the past few years the big players – Compass, Granada and Sodexho Gardner Merchant – have been swallowing up middle sized players to such an extent that Nelson Hind is now the last national independent food caterer left. "Our industry is becoming polarized," says Nelson. "On the one hand you have the Granadas and the Compasses, where the service is increasingly standardized and centralized. On the other, you have tiny operations with star chefs such as Ramsay MacDonald offering higher and higher quality on a one-off basis."

Nelson Hind is fighting to combine scale with the specialist's touch. It runs 220 contracts across Britain with customers ranging from a Derbyshire quarry to Charterhouse public school and Rolls-Royce's London head office. No two operations are the same. Chefs design their own menus, do their own purchasing, much of it local and seasonal, and run their units as small businesses. The formula has been successful, with customers valuing the freshness of the food and the flexibility of the service, and Nelson Hind has grown it at 70 per cent per year for many years. But with increasing size – it had sales of £26 million last year – this service gets harder to provide. "It's easy to innovate when your small," says Nelson. "But it gets harder as you grow. Most independent food services sell out once they reach a certain size. They are seduced by offers from bigger players." He cites Baxter and Platts, which supplies high quality catering services to City firms. But having reached sales of £26 million its owners sold last year to Granada.

With the middle ground fast eroding, Nelson Hind faces an identity crisis. It cannot go back to its early cavalier days when Nelson and his partner Chris Hind, now executive chairman, were troubleshooting across a swathe of England that stretched from their head office in Rugby to East Anglia. Today he runs a national network with contracts fairly evenly distributed from Glasgow to Poole. Nelson does not want to go down the standardization road. But to continue providing services on a national scale presents big logistics, staffing and management problems. "We run each contract as an individual operation. And there is a high administration cost for every contract," he says. He did, for instance, do customer research when he won the contract to supply the Royal National Institute for the Blind. This led him to supply dishes without garnishes and on plates with high rims.

Nelson Hind has invested heavily in information technology over the past two years to manage the ever increasing volume of data. It has converted its head office basement into an accounts department, but it can do nothing about one key source of complexity: the number of suppliers. With 85 per cent of ingredients fresh, and chefs doing their purchasing. Nelson's company sales ledger has about 3,500 suppliers for 220 operations. Most companies of its size would find these numbers too high. But for Nelson Hind individual purchasing is a bedrock principle. "Involving the catering manager in the purchase of food removes any barrier to that manager being held responsible for the quality of the food," says Nelson. "It is fundamental. If you are telling them what to buy and where to buy from, how can you hold them accountable when standards drop?"

Having fresh spinach soup in the Derbyshire quarry and locally grown caramelized baby carrots at Rolls-Royce is nice for the customer, but when Nelson Hind competes in a tender it is bidding for business against companies that have centralized purchasing, with everything that implies in economies of scale and the relative ease of replicating operations. Even when Granada "keeps the shop front in place" after an acquisition, the acquired company will usually be benefiting from standardized purchasing, menu and product design, branding and service. Nelson and Hind decided long ago they had no interest running a catering business based on standardization. They left senior positions at the Sutcliffe catering company to start their own business when Sutcliffe was sold by Peninsular and Orient to Granada in 1990.

"Standardization is the obvious route to go down to make more money," says Nelson. "But then you are focused purely on margins and not on the product. Frankly it gets boring." The price of their approach is weaker margins. On sales of £26 million last year, the company made a pre-tax profit of £1.2 million. Its margins have consistently averaged about 4 per cent when the industry average has been 10 per cent and a player such as Granada can make 12–14 per cent. Although he could easily bump up the bottom line by cutting the bespoke service, rationalizing suppliers and reducing head count, Nelson does not believe this is in the company's long-term interest. "We have grown by offering a higher cost product at a relatively low price. Our service is quality driven and personal with a higher proportion of people to clients. We could bump up profits in the short term but in the longer term I believe this is how we will continue to grow." But even after accepting lower margins than rivals, the directors are finding the operational side of the business harder to manage. "Chris and I are under pressure," says Nelson. "Performing on 10 to 20 sites is difficult. But doing this on 200 sites is something else altogether. But if we abandon our policy what has this company got left?"

Clearly, scale demands the delegation of responsibility downwards. Here too, decentralization reveals itself as a demanding policy. Nelson Hind depends heavily on its core staff: the chefs or catering managers. They have to be multi-skilled: they must be creative in the kitchen, they must manage an independent business unit, and they must sell, co-operating with clients to maximize the value of an existing contract and selling the service to others in the area. In the 1990 recession, when the company was launched, it benefited from a weakness in the hotel and restaurant trades because it could attract good chefs at reasonable prices. Having worked in proprietor-led restaurants or hotels, these chefs had experience of designing menus, purchasing and managing autonomous commercial operations. They were used to showing initiative, working without notice and operating to tight deadlines. But the picture is now different. The 1990s restaurant boom has produced a nation-wide shortage of the people Nelson Hind needs. This competition is most severe in London, but it is also apparent in other areas. Although the company can compete with the restaurant trade by offering good salaries, job security and a genuinely five day working week, it cannot compete with the glamour of a successful restaurant. The rise of the celebrity chef has meant that most ambitious young chefs seek their training in a renowned restaurant, not in a catering contract operation.

Parallel with this labor shortage, Nelson has identified a "de-skilling" of the industry, caused by standardization and the erosion of training standards. Big centralized operations with command and control structures do not demand so much from their staff. "It is much easier to communicate messages to a less skilled workforce," says Nelson. "Someone working in MacDonald's has to learn how to turn the chip pan on and judge when the chips are done. They don't have to know how to make short crust pastry or a béchamel sauce, how to do cash flow analysis or sell a contract to a new client."

Nelson has tried to solve his staffing problem by promoting people from within. He has focused on offering opportunities to energetic, resourceful people who might not otherwise been given them. "If, for example, you take on a woman returning to the workplace after having children, someone who has no formal qualifications but lots of life skills, and you give her training, you can find a valuable member of staff," he says. "She will often show great reserves of energy and loyalty." But this still does not solve the problem entirely. Nelson Hind has now reached a size where it is becoming well known and is being invited to bid for business it would not have been considered for before. It is actually turning down contracts because it could not risk not having the staff to honor them to the required standard. A sign of this is the fact that it has recently diverted some sales staff to operations. But putting the brakes on growth also has drawbacks. Good people are attracted to the company because dynamic growth creates opportunity. The Nelson Hind car park overflows with new customized A4 Audis. It offers competitive pay packages and in-house training. But Nelson acknowledges that loyalty does not come from financial inducements alone.

Nelson says: "Retaining the best people depends on providing a field for their ambition – you have to grow the company so they have somewhere to go. The pace of growth is not necessarily led by Chris and me. It is led by the ambitions of the staff and this makes the company culture harder to hold together." As you take on more business, there is an upward suck of good staff and you are left with a vacuum again. I think that's why so many people sell up. They get tired of the never-ending cycle."

Acknowledgements: Sarah Gracie, *The Enterprise Network. The Sunday Times*, June 27, 1999

TASK

Assume that you have accepted the job of Chief Executive at Nelson Hind and that your contract includes a substantial bonus that is related to bottom line performance and a 15 per cent share in the business to be awarded at the end of three years. Use Fig. 1.1 to capture your initial thoughts about how to make a success of the job. You should make one "tick" against each proposition.

Figure 1.1 Identifying what drives your business performance

Propositions about how to make a success of your job at Nelson Hind	Strongly support +3	+2	+1	No view 0	−1	−2	Strongly against −3	Total
1 My focus will be on central control.								
2 We will clarify our policies and rules then communicate them to all staff.								
3 I want to see clear goals and plans.								
4 I want to deliver Nelson's vision.								
5 Our success depends on having simple business processes in place.								
6 We will concentrate on clients that can provide high margins.								
7 We will set up businesss divisions and promote competition between them.								
8 I want a 5-year plan and will then stick to it.								
9 I will make cost-cutting a way of life.								
10 It would not be wise to seek business outside the UK.								
11 We must cut back on innovation and promote the intangibles in the brand image.								
12 We will focus on the long-term strategies and let the short term take care of itself.								
13 I want volume growth and managers to stop worrying about adding more value.								
14 We must grow by taking small steps and checking our progress carefully.								
15 The strategies for growth will come from a clear focus and from doing more of the same.								
16 The rules of play must override any personal beliefs that managers have about how to run the business.								
17 The future will depend on in-house competences and we are not going to outsource.								

There are two distinct drivers behind your approach to understanding and taking action in business situations. The first of these is the degree to which you seek to impose central control or favor local autonomy. The second is the extent to which your approach is one of low risk and uses traditional and conservative thinking or one where you are prepared to break the mold and take risks. To discover how wedded you are to the notions of central control or to local autonomy first add up your total score for propositions **1–8**.

Score +24 to +15

You certainly like to be in control. Have you ever thought of running a steel works? There is nothing wrong with this approach. Having clear directives supported by a strong culture focused on efficiency and meeting performance targets is often a recipe for success. A company such as Nelson Hind does not appear to have taken this route so far. But all the signs are that competition is fierce and that margins will continue to be challenged. Delivering short-term results while achieving Nelson's vision will require some luck but at least you will not have to out-guess the owners. Relying on business processes, concentrating on contribution and promoting some healthy competition sounds like a formula that would have made you popular at Harvard in the 1970s and 1980s. Following clear plans, and sticking to them, while resisting the temptation to chase the odd rabbit sounds like good business sense. Your approach suggests that you favor a task perspective which, if carried to an extreme, could result in Nelson Hind being an obdurate and oppressive company to work for. I am sure that you would deny this.

Score +14 to +5

You like control but are prepared to incorporate some balance and flexibility when faced with strategic decisions. As the company is growing fast you see the value of controlling key business decisions but recognize that local autonomy may be essential and not just a luxury. Also you recognize the need to share learning although not at the expense of developing a laissez-faire culture. You want to see plans but also accept that chaos may occasionally be the reality for local managers. Holding the corporate line is seen as important but you would also welcome some original and challenging thinking from your managers. But not too much and only when you feel that it is appropriate. You would support the managers who wanted to keep delighting their clients but would restrict their independence when margins are threatened. You are prepared to let your managers share their learning but want to encourage some competition to keep them focused on success. Run this way Nelson Hind could be a company that stays where it is and with good luck might survive for some years. Which is what you wanted to happen.

Score +4 to –5

If you are stuck in the middle then perhaps you should go back to the questions or the story and let your true feelings take over. Have another go. It is not that I am looking for extremes but often strategists find that they are ambivalent about a particular business. There is nothing wrong with this but the conventional wisdom suggests that when this is the case then they have little to contribute. In which case they should, quite rightly, say and do very little. To be successful a strategist has to have some fire and commitment. If it is not there then look for another arena, one in which you have some strong feelings.

Score –6 to –14

You like the business dynamics to drive the company but want to still be able to get at the steering wheel. You see local autonomy being tempered with control. You want your managers to learn in areas that you believe will help you meet performance targets. By creating stretch targets, for your managers, you expect them to find new ways of tackling business growth and margin management. But you want to set the pace. Sharing knowledge among the managers will be encouraged but once again you want to set up the learning processes and make sure that there is a direct link back to business performance. Adding value through business processes will be your aim but the objective must be to satisfy the client needs once the contract is signed. Run this way the company is likely to prosper but you may find, as you probably have already, that it is very demanding to keep the exploration perspective going. The tendency will be for the momentum that this approach creates to move the organization into an unstable state.

Score –15 to –24

You like local autonomy and the entrepreneur stills burns strong in your soul. But you see Nelson Hind benefiting from having an open culture and managers who thrive on chaos. By concentrating on continuing to give your customers value for money, even at the expense of margin, you expect success. You will encourage your managers to seek every opportunity to delight the customers and in this way lead the company into new markets and service offerings. Your habits are creating what I call an exploration, as opposed to a task, perspective, expecting and allowing new and unexpected things to happen. You are a no rules manager and cutting out any bureaucracy is your forte. For you, competition between managers at Nelson Hind would be totally inappropriate. If carried to an extreme, then your habits will turn Nelson Hind into a company that is at best seen as egocentric and at worst unstable. But then that may be what you are trying to achieve. The company would either excel or self destruct. At least it would be exciting and is an approach that organizations, in turbulent times, are encouraged to adopt.

To explore the other aspect of your approach add up your total score for propositions **9–17**. This will indicate whether your approach is conventional and based on a low level of risk taking or change driven and involves taking high risks.

Score +27 to +14

You would stand out as a perfect product of the conventional thinker school. Chasing down the costs, with a clear focus on local businesses while promoting a clear message about brand value. Yours would be seen as a welcome approach by the owners. A determination to win an increasing share of a targeted market with innovations based on sound feedback as to their relevance being preferred over making radical changes. Tried and tested approaches to delivering the service would be encouraged within a tight set of rules and procedures. Developing in-house skills and competences would be seen as your recipe for success. With this approach your efforts would be to take Nelson Hind to a position where all risk had been eliminated.

Score +13 to 0

You are still in favor of following the management conventions about how best to compete. But you would temper cost cutting with a concern for maintaining the quality that Nelson Hind had used to grow the business. Your vision for the company would include a time horizon beyond the end of year and customer care would figure highly in your approach to growing the business. Maintaining the customer base would be paramount. Outsourcing of some of the activities would figure in your thinking and be balanced with a concern to build on core competences.

Score –1 to –14

Your concern to grow the company would involve you in a degree of risk taking. Certainly being prepared to look outside of existing markets and services. Customer care and quality would figure high on your agenda as ways of growing the business. You would also be prepared to encourage the more radical thinking managers in the business. An approach that favored a breadth of vision rather than offering focused strategies would become a hallmark of your style.

Score –15 to –27

Here you are showing all your tendencies to break with convention. You seek opportunity and change in all situations. Global growth, promotion of quality beyond imagination, and a focus on a stretching vision of the future for Nelson Hind would mark you out as a revolutionary. Customers would receive an enormous amount of attention and be encouraged to shape and influence the service offering to suit their requirements. Your view would be that growth will come from delighting the clients, finding new market opportunities and gaining higher margins in the process. Radical change would quickly become your middle name. Networking with suppliers and even competitors would certainly be part of your approach to achieving your ambitions for the company and yourself. Taken to these extremes the company would be driven by a series of high risk strategies. The rewards could be enormous and the downside disaster.

This review is likely to have confirmed your own preconceptions of how best to approach strategy making in a complex situation. Alternatively, where it has challenged your thinking or if you are unhappy with the way that you appear to be approaching the game, then take heart. I will show you in the next section how these approaches to the use of control and risk taking in business management are applied by some of the best game players.

The rules of the game

For most of us games tend to be pleasurable. We all have our favorite pastimes and the sports industry rivals the turnover of some of the largest industrial corporations. But how useful is it to view business development as a form of competitive game, a game played between people like you, who work in organizations and are probably totally unaware of each other's actions? Unfortunately the pay-off from your decision to make a price reduction or to launch a new product often depends more on the reactions of competitors than customers. But competitors may be totally oblivious to your moves and simply be applying their own recipes for success. Faced with a small number of players, as in the case of Nelson Hind above, there are two approaches to making sense of how the game is being played: game theory and behavioral theory.

Game theory

In game theory there are two major considerations. The first is where two businesses are locked in competition and what one loses the other gains. This is known as the zero-sum game. Business A would assume that B would exploit any situation to maximum advantage. A's strategy is therefore to ensure that any outcomes of a strategic decision would provide minimum advantage to B. With this approach A would be making the best of a bad job and giving B the worst of a good job. Fortunately in most business situations there is scope for co-operation as well as competition. This second, much more common approach, is known as non-zero-sum game theory. This can include freewheeling, where the bargaining is unrestricted, and rule-based games. With the rule-based approach the challenge is one of mapping your strategic actions against those of the competitors in terms of quantifiable pay-offs. The results are often presented in the form of a decision matrix. As in all representations there is a need to fix the values of certain parameters and to reduce the uncertainties, the aim being to produce a robust but insightful model. Perfection is definitely not the name of this game.

Behavioral theory

Behavioral theory looks at game-playing at an organizational level and not at that of the individual. The argument is that the dynamics created by an organization's history will determine its behavior. The inertia created by senior managers, capabilities, stakeholders, networks of relationships and the core values and beliefs of the organization combine to create the organizational dynamics. Our own experiences also tell us that commitment to a strategy can sometimes be driven from an emotional rather than an objective or analytic approach. The appearance of irrational behavior where managers attempt to justify choices and use selective arguments to support self-serving decisions, plus the inevitable personality clashes, all introduce a bias into the game. A bias that is very difficult to second guess.

> Behavioral theory looks at game-playing at an organizational level and not at that of the individual

The value in understanding game theory and behavioral theory is in recognizing the power of their combination. But even with this combination, the approach is only of use where there are only a few players and we have a lot of detailed information about the areas where decisions are to be made. The situation that most business managers face is having to play the game when there are many organizations and many players; about whom very little is known.

Playing the game

The conventional approach to playing the competitive business game is one of positioning in the marketplace, combining both attack and defense. Competitive advantage is created by providing customers with recognizable added value and being able to influence the structure of the industry and the marketplace. Organizations also use product and process innovation to gain competitive advantage, both of which are vulnerable to being imitated or copied. In some situations these innovations will help grow the size of the overall market. But the long-term effect will be to drive down prices and destroy profitability for both the originator and the imitator. New entrants then move in with a new business model, or a set of offerings, that supersedes those being used by the present incumbents. There are many ways in which organizations combat imitation but at a cost in management time and energy. Such attacks are a constant distraction to managers who are trying to maximize their margins by improving operational processes. A further challenge is to defend against substitute products and services being brought into the market. This can be even more endemic where the substitution takes the form of a new way of doing business. An example of this has been where the introduction of e-business has resulted in restructuring of both industries and markets. Learned approaches to resource development and market positioning strategies are having to be completely revised.

Experience tells us that business development results from the thinking and action of individuals. At one level we have the corporate power figures who are able to make far-reaching decisions that impact on the business, such as takeovers and mergers. While at another level there are thousands of business and operational managers who are engaged daily in taking actions that have a cumulative impact on the business direction. We would like to believe that there is a close link between the corporate strategists' decisions and the actions of the local business managers, but a moment's reflection tells us that this is unrealistic. The notion that there is a seamless link has been kept alive by managers who cannot deal with the consequences of accepting that the link may not exist. So where does that leave us?

Four game plays

In this book, competitive game playing is made personal. We do this by studying the perspectives held by the players involved in both managing and developing the business. They do this while having to live with pressures from others, both within and outside the organization. We must also remember that these managers are like you. They are not automotans. They have aspirations, fears, jobs and careers to manage. By looking at the perspectives held about the business itself, we can start to see how game plays will vary. Figure 1.2 illustrates how these perspectives can dominate the business development game that individuals are prepared to play.

There are two key dimensions that structure the available game plays. The first is where the player is quite clear that the purpose and objective of the game is to achieve measurable business outcomes such as return on investment or greater market share, and at the other extreme where the outcomes are more hidden and unclear. At this extreme are multiple objectives, many of which are not easily quantifiable, e.g. staying in business and continuing to pursue personal ambitions. The second dimension is characterized, at one extreme, by a confidence that outcomes are definable and determinable, while at the other, the manager accepts that the business environment is chaotic and that managing this chaos is a reality and also an opportunity. In quadrant 1 the approach taken by the manager is to plan and take actions based on a detailed analysis of the environment and the local business capability and then to implement those decisions that best satisfy the requirements and strengths of the business. This is a conventional and well loved way of playing the business development game.

Figure 1.2 Four perspectives on playing the business development game

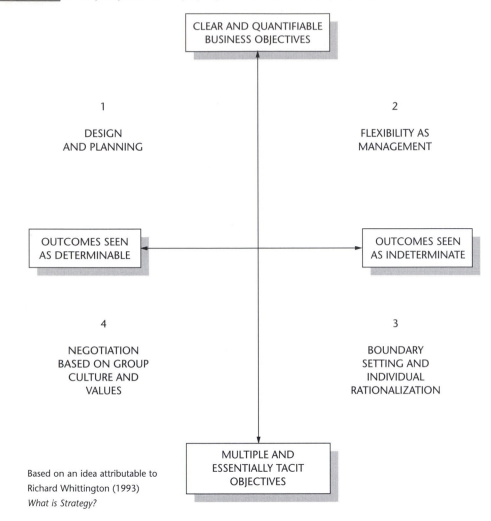

CLEAR AND QUANTIFIABLE
BUSINESS OBJECTIVES

1

DESIGN
AND PLANNING

2

FLEXIBILITY AS
MANAGEMENT

OUTCOMES SEEN
AS DETERMINABLE

OUTCOMES SEEN
AS INDETERMINATE

4

NEGOTIATION
BASED ON GROUP
CULTURE AND
VALUES

3

BOUNDARY
SETTING AND
INDIVIDUAL
RATIONALIZATION

Based on an idea attributable to
Richard Whittington (1993)
What is Strategy?

MULTIPLE AND
ESSENTIALLY TACIT
OBJECTIVES

In quadrant 2 we have the manager who has identified some clear out-comes that are quantifiable, but who has accepted that the environment and other people's actions, both inside and outside the business, are unpre-dictable. Uncertainty is embraced and the manager relies more on oppor-tunism than on planned action and reaction. This is the quadrant in which the entrepreneur is likely to be found. Although this manager is also able to move from chaos to certainty and back to chaos without a great deal of stress. Flexibility is the hallmark of this manager.

Quadrant 3 is dominated by the manager who sets boundaries that are based on a rationalization over the links between action and outcomes. Here there are multiple objectives, many of which are hidden or implicit to the way the manager behaves. There is also an acceptance that the external and internal business environments cannot be controlled. The game becomes one where sufficing predominates. Many managers find themselves driven into this quadrant as a result of their failure to survive in quadrants 1 or 2.

In quadrant 4 we find the manager who has some strongly held beliefs about the reason why the business should exist and what it should really be focusing on. A view that may well be at odds with the direction being promoted by the corporate agenda. This individual may be leading a senior management team that represent a strong cultural group or be determined to change the way in which the industry is structured.

The complexity of how to play the business development game is often compounded by the range of perspectives that exist both within one company and among competing companies. This complexity has a tendency to polarize the game players into operating in one of the quadrants that most suit the industry. For example, in the steel industry, quadrant 1 appears to dominate, whereas in the non-government agencies, where there are mixed objectives that have a strong value base, quadrant 4 players might be more common. As you begin to develop an overarching strategy that links your personal agenda to that of the corporation, knowing your position among these quadrants becomes key. Equally important is then checking that your position is realistic, in terms of balancing your personal ambitions with the need to gain support from those in the organization that are responsible to the stakeholders for business performance. This does not mean that I am advocating blind obedience to the corporate credo, but neither am I recommending that organizations are places for individuals to do as they please with someone else's money. The skill is in being able to strike a balance that more than satisfies the expectations of all parties.

As you can see, we have the bones of a complex and challenging set of options from which to choose how we play the business game. It is time that we looked at some recognized champions at play.

Who are the key players and what makes them so?

The job of a Chief Executive has historically been to create the vision, confirm the strategy, put in place a hierarchical structure, hire and appoint key people, establish self-sufficient businesses and make sure that controls are in place. This is known as the "Alfred Sloan model" and still underpins a great deal of the thinking and game playing that corporate leaders engage in. Jack Welch at General Electric challenged this top down approach in the early 1980s with his determination to preach and implement empowerment. His aim was to create a customer facing organization. Here the Chief Executive focuses on:

- restructuring (downsizing and de-layering)
- reducing bureaucratic behavior
- giving employees freedom to decide and act
- creating an atmosphere where continuous improvement becomes the norm.

The thrust of this approach is to change underlying beliefs that staff hold about the purpose of the organization and how it should operate. There have been a few casualties arising from over zealous application of this empowerment approach. The losses at Barings when Nick Leeson was given free rein, and the massive losses that General Electric experienced at Kidder Peabody are examples of where letting go at the top has resulted in disaster.

Corporate growth through takeovers and asset stripping became the game to play in the 1970s and 1980s. But failure to sustain the meteoric growth which resulted from this type of strategy led to a search for new ways of playing the growth game. Forming strategic alliances in order to create synergistic outcomes has now become the current formula for success. Companies that we know as household names now have hundreds of formal alliances, many with companies that previously would have been classed as their arch competitors. These links also extend to suppliers. For example, Ford Motor Company, along with its rivals, now has much closer relationships with suppliers and see them as part of its design and manufacturing resource. This form of collaboration also extends to sharing of information systems, customer and market profiling. A typical example here is where KPMG have formed alliances with CISCO and Compaq as a way of tackling the market for e-business services.

> Forming strategic alliances in order to create synergistic outcomes has now become the current formula for success

Whether you work in a small, medium or large, private or public sector organization, it is vital to understand where and how the power figures are driving the organization. A recent study by Michael Goold, Andrew Campbell and Marcus Alexander into the strategic thinking frameworks used in leading organizations, gives some clues to the pattern behind the game playing of the power group. To understand the game plays we are advised to follow three steps.

1. Understand the type of business that is the focus of the strategy. Identify the key players in the industry, the dominant technology and the features of the markets.
2. Understand the nature of the business opportunities that are being sought and how success is being defined and evaluated.
3. Understand the intentions and habits of the key power figures who are driving the business growth, recognizing that these intentions suggest one of three distinctive organizational styles.

Three organizational styles

First, a style that emphasizes strategic goals and competitive positioning being less concerned with centralized financial control. Blue-chip companies such as British Petroleum Amoco, now a $10 billion company, Cadbury Schweppes, Banc One and Canon were all categorized as exhibiting this style. Their focus is on using a formalized strategic planning process to seek consensus between the ambitions of the corporate group and the subsidiary businesses. In these firms the business managers were rewarded more as a result of the health of the overall group than on the performance of their own business.

Second, a style where the focus is on balancing financial targets with strategic targets. Companies such as 3M, Asea Brown Boveri, RTZ, Unilever, ICI and Courtaulds were grouped in this category. Here the short-term goals were being balanced with a more strategic approach. The subsidiary businesses were encouraged to work within broad guidelines set by corporate-level directives. The role of the directors being to question rather than to dictate the decisions. The emphasis is on decentralization of decision making around strategies with financial targets being balanced with the achievement of strategic milestones.

The third style emphasizes tight financial control and short-term performance is rewarded. Falling into this group are BTR, GEC, Tarmac and Hanson. Here the pursuit of financial control predominates. The subsidiaries are expected to structure their own business and to survive or fail through the pursuit of their own market, or resource-based strategies. There is little evidence of a formalized central strategy-making process. Capital investment decisions have to be approved by the corporate group and control is through a tight monitoring of performance against annual budgets. But our researchers provided perhaps one of the most vital clues to our quest to resolve the strategy enigma with the following extract:

> The parenting style of a company follows from the basic beliefs of the parenting team about how relationships between the parent and the business should be handled, and about how the parent can add most value. It reflects the experience, philosophy, and values of the chief executive and his or her team. As such, it is deeply ingrained and difficult to alter. We have found that companies seldom voluntarily change in style, and, over time, a gradual evolution of a company's style can occur. But a planned move from one style to another, without a major shift in the composition of the top team, is rare.

> Goold, M., Campbell, A. and Alexander, M. *Corporate Level Strategy;*
> *Creating Value in the Multibusiness Company*

This quotation suggests that the way in which business development games are played depends on the experiences and ingrained approaches of the people in the power group. Understanding how the games are being played by the power figures in your own organization will help you to determine your own strategy. A personal strategy that takes account of the overall game being played by the corporation but in a way that does not reduce your chances of satisfying your ambitions and work performance. Developing an understanding of your ingrained approaches to business development and how they can be changed to improve your work performance is one of the key aims of this book. But in order to do this we first need to look a bit more closely at some of the core beliefs and approaches of those who profess to understand the business development game.

Understanding how the games are being played by the power figures in your own organization will help you to determine your own strategy

2

Some fundamental
beliefs about business success

We can believe what we choose. We are answerable for
what we choose to believe.

Cardinal Newman (1801–1890) British Theologian

What can the gurus tell us?

Competitiveness and rivalry are the foundation stones of the core beliefs of
the entrepreneur and business developer. The advice on how to succeed in
business and in life falls into two camps. On the one hand we are told to
model our behavior on successful individuals and imitate their approach to
developing a business. A message that is promoted in the media, management
and business magazines. Becoming a *"me too"* will always be a popular theme.
At the other extreme we are encouraged to be mavericks. To break out and to
create our own unique approach and develop a set of capabilities that are
ahead of the competition and difficult to imitate. This presents us with a
dilemma over whether to focus or break out.

It will come as no surprise to hear that this dilemma is dealt with by allowing the dynamics of rivalry, in the business setting, to reach a natural state of
equilibrium. By dynamics I mean the effect that results when one player
makes a competitive move. The rules of engagement are clear to those who are
experienced in the industry and after time the plays are easily defined and
usually predictable. The players, by colluding in this way, either tacitly or
explicitly, create a state where protection from outsiders is a key part of their
game play. This allows them to concentrate on competition between a known
set of players, using well-developed rules. The outcomes are, within reasonable limits, predictable by all the players. The danger comes when either one
player decides to change their beliefs about how the game is to be played or
outside events, beyond their control, change the factors that made the game
worth playing.

This notion that industries can be described as constituting competitive
strategic groups is well established and underpins the core beliefs of the

entrepreneur and business developer. The belief is that strategic groups can be found by looking for those that are pursuing similar strategies and using similar measures of performance. This notion of strategic groups has led to the popularity of evaluative techniques such as competitor benchmarking. But researchers have also invented the term "primary competitive groups" to describe those organizations that see each other as immediate rivals. These primary groups are seen as having a shared mind-set about how to compete and what levels of success are to be expected. An analogy here is that ducks feeding in a pond work in strategic groups, whereas seagulls following a fishing trawler act more like primary groups. The battle is swift and unforgiving when compared with the much more cosy arrangement developed by the ducks. This is a key distinction and one that we need to take a closer look at if we are to grasp this core belief about achieving success in a competitive world.

The gurus tell us that there are two basic approaches to achieving a position of sustainable competitive advantage for a business. With the first approach we are advised to position the company in the marketplace in terms of market share and customer perception of the added value that it provides. Then to keep a close watch on our competitors' attempts to challenge that position, matching and reacting to both market threats and opportunities using a mix of generic strategies.

An alternative approach involves adopting a resource-based perspective. Here we are encouraged to focus on core competences within the organization and how these can be combined to create capabilities that are unique and not easily copied. Then we are to find ways of adding value to our customer offerings by applying these capabilities.

Both of these approaches eventually involve deciding who our competitors are and what response they are likely to make to our strategic moves. This reinforces the earlier point made about competitive groups. We can either identify competitive groups using explicit measures of their strategies and the outcomes, or we can look at groups of companies that share the same mental models of how the game has to be played. As our behavior is so dependent on who we see as our competitors, being able to recognize whether we are identifying them as strategic groups or primary groups becomes imperative. You may wish to reflect, for a moment, on who you consider to be your key business competitors and what type of grouping they represent.

The gurus also tell us that business strategists hold distinctive views on what determines how managers approach and play the strategy game. If we are to understand the moves of the other players then we have to be able to recognize these distinctive views and compare them to our own. The views are concerned with:

- what business strategy really is
- where it comes from

- the extent to which it can be predetermined
- the extent to which business strategy results from overt competitive moves between companies.

The guru that holds most sway in this area is Henry Mintzberg. His seminal works *The Rise and Fall of Strategic Planning* and *Strategy Safari* have been a great influence on the way strategists think and we need to glean what we can from his efforts.

Henry Mintzberg's ten schools of thought

Mintzberg has identified ten schools of thought or points of view on strategy formation; these are illustrated in Fig. 2.1. The first three are prescriptive and are concerned with describing how strategies should be formed. The rest are concerned with trying to explain the processes involved when managers are engaged in the complexity of strategic management. We begin by looking at three prescriptive schools.

Designers

The first of these, the design school, is based on the view that the strategist can use an analytical approach to find out how to match the organization's strengths and weaknesses to opportunities and threats in the business environment. Then by identifying the critical success factors essential to competing successfully in that industry, a range of possible strategies can be identified. Selection of the best strategies can then be made using criteria such as risk, return, competitive advantage and feasibility. The implementation of these strategies is then managed through a balance of organizational structure, performance measures and financial controls. This viewpoint is one where actions are driven by the corporate management or the Chief Executive. The main criticisms made against the design viewpoint are that, first, thinking should not be separated from action, and second, the strengths of the organization have to be tested in the context of an external environment that is in a constant state of change.

Planners

The second school in our "how to" category is centered on the strategic or business planning process. Here the corporate group set out the long-term goals or objectives of the enterprise. Then an audit of the external and internal environment is completed using an approach similar to that of the design school. A range of strategies are then determined and evaluated in order to assess the extent to which they present a risk against desired returns. The evaluation is heavily biased towards the use of financial performance

Figure 2.1 **Perspectives on strategy formulation**

How strategies are derived	
By design	SWOT/critical success factors/matching to the business context
From a planning process	Long term objectives/financial criteria/plans/budgets
By positioning	Industry analysis/value chains/competition/strategic groups/game theory/generic strategies/Boston Grid
Perspectives adopted by strategists	
Entrepreneurial	Individuals with a business idea/a search for opportunities/calculated risk taking/corporate renewal/creation of a strategic architecture
Cognitive	Mental models/maps/metaphor/peronality/cognitive styles
Learning	Logical incrementalism/handling uncertainty and ambiguity/innovation and corporate venturing/tacit and explicit knowledge/core competences
Power and Politics	Balancing shareholders and stakeholders/internal and external negotiations/positional power/joint ventures and alliances/networks
Cultural	Shared beliefs/organizational paradigm/managing change
Environmentalist	External factors dictate the strategic options/survival of the most adaptable/strategic options limited by regulation/imitation/expert opinion
Configuration	Organizations move between stable and unstable conditions/industry and business lifecycles/structure follows strategy

Adapted from ideas contained in *Strategy Safari*, Mintzberg H., Ahlstrand B. and Lampel J. (1998) Prentice Hall.

metrics. The planning school relies on a total process that starts with a set of objectives and culminates with a set of plans, budgets and controls that can be implemented by the businesses. Much of the criticism of this school has been around the inability of the planners to forecast, when faced with an uncertain future, with enough accuracy to make planning a realistic activity. Researchers have shown that forecasting environments and competitors' actions beyond two years is notoriously inaccurate. Dealing with this criticism has resulted in efforts to focus on scenarios or possible futures into which the current business ideas and associated strategies are then mapped. In this way the corporate planners use the design process to heighten the ability of the business managers to anticipate and pre-empt changes as opposed to simply reacting when things fail to work to plan.

Positioning

The third and most popular school of "how to" is that of positioning made famous by Michael Porter in his book *Competitive Strategy*. The basic idea is quite simple. If a firm can apply two or three generic strategies, such as price, differentiation of products or services or agree a market focus, then it will be able to achieve a position of sustainable competitive advantage, creating the resources and wealth that will enable it to invest further and grow. Knowing when and how to apply these generic strategies depended, so Porter argues, on being able to conduct a detailed analysis of the firm's environment and the marketplace. Understanding the industry structure is the key for this positioning school and techniques such as value chain analysis and the Boston Consulting matrix, with the infamous cash cow have all won their place in the hearts and minds of devotees of this perspective. Positioning also draws on lessons learned from the military. The writings of warriors such as Sun Tzu, captured in the best seller, *Art of War*, 1971, provide a great deal of support for strategies and game playing that rely on being able to anticipate and upstage your opponents.

There has been much criticism of the positioning school and this is primarily around the question of it tending to restrict the creative work of the strategist. That an over-emphasis on analysis, as opposed to seeking a unique or breakthrough idea, encourages a "formula-based" approach to strategy making.

We now need to look at the processes involved when managers engage in the complexity of business development. They are conveniently categorized as representing schools of strategic thinking.

Entrepreneurs

The first of these schools of strategic thinking tells us that winning strategies follow from the vision and imagination of the entrepreneurial leader. The emphasis here is on the leader who has a unique business idea about how to create wealth. Bill Gates of Microsoft, Richard Branson of Virgin Group and many other famous business founders are held up as epitomizing this school. Much of the research into this perspective has been focused on identifying the characteristics and personality of the entrepreneurial leader. Mintzberg has suggested four characteristics of the entrepreneur as a strategy maker:

- their sense of urgency in searching for new opportunities
- their total hold on the organizational power

- an ability to take bold decisions when faced with uncertainty
- a total focus on growth.

Many people believe that entrepreneurs only succeed in particular circumstances, for example, in start-up situations or where an organization is facing renewal. But a growing view is that many entrepreneurs are driven by a desire to create the architecture that will enable an organization to handle complexity and change. Suggesting that they take a much longer term view of how the business needs to develop than we give them credit for.

Cognition

The cognitive school argues that strategists form mental models, or cognitive maps, that are then used to direct action. Further, that there are biases around how judgements are made, about what is fact and what information is ambiguous and uncertain. If strategists are to make sense of their own maps and those being used by others then they have to engage in some form of representation and interaction. The representation is usually carried out by the use of metaphor or analogy and in doing this have to contend with their own, and their colleagues', personalities and cognitive style. This quest to understand bias and cognitive style has resulted in many managers being made aware of their Myers Briggs rating. Here the manager is assumed to approach problem identification and solution on the bases of either valuing the "big picture" or "detailed facts," valuing thinking processes or relying on emotions and feelings to find solutions to strategic issues. Unfortunately this approach has a tendency to induce a fatalistic rather than an enquiring approach to handling differences in style.

Learning

The learning school takes the view that strategies emerge over time and that learning takes place in the minds of the players. The assumption is that there is a link between learning and subsequent action. Learning thus becomes continuous and is both planned and ad hoc. James Quinn has been attributed to coining the phrase "logical incrementalism" as a way of capturing this notion. Here we see a break with the traditional belief that strategy can be formulated by analysis and decision making based on hard data. The view taken is that strategy is being continuously developed through the actions of many people and that this activity transcends the organizational structures. But Quinn did not throw formal and directive strategy making to the winds. He suggested that there was still an overarching but loosely defined pattern or direction that was set by top management.

The difference between this view and that of the prescriptive school is that here players in the organization are encouraged to help the pattern develop. At an organizational level the learning school also claims ownership for what has become known as "corporate venturing." This is where key players or venture managers are charged with developing new strategic initiatives for the business. Venturing can include initiating research into new product and service offerings, or exploring a possible change in direction for the organization. Here we have the notion that the business managers should concentrate on running their existing business ideas to maximum efficiency while being confident that their future is being managed through this venturing process. With all learning there is the issue of how to make tacit learning, that which exists at the subconscious level, visible and usable by others. How to make tacit knowledge explicit has been a major focus for researchers such as Nonaka and Takeuchi and described in their book *The Knowledge Creating Company*. Here those who are engaged in making strategy go through successive stages of:

- *socialization* (where tacit knowledge is shared and mental models exposed)
- *externalization* (where new models are created and shared at the explicit level using language)
- *combination* (where these explicit models are shared with others in the organization as a way of testing for authenticity and relevance)
- *internalization* (where the new and shared learning is translated into the language of the organization and embedded in key procedures. This puts the shared learning back into the tacit mode and action taking becomes routinized as an organizational capability).

The final contribution from the school of learning is the notion that core competences exist within organizations as a set of skills, knowledge and experiences and that these core competences can then be put together in unique ways to establish capabilities which, in turn, are matched to opportunities for adding value for customers in the marketplace. This notion, championed by gurus such as Gary Hamel and Keith Prahalad, depends for its success on a clear statement of strategic intent and a determination to achieve a strategic fit between the capabilities and the competitive environment. To qualify as a core competence, the argument is that the collective learning of the organization must:

The learning school has been criticized for purporting to be all things to all men

- be potentially applicable to a number of markets
- add significant value to the end customer or user
- be difficult to imitate or copy.

The learning school has been criticized for purporting to be all things to all men, and taking the rationality out of business management. But it does show us how to grapple with the uncertain and ambiguous aspects that we face when trying to predict future business outcomes. Perhaps it is the glue that holds our rational world together, or at least our concern that it must be rational. It is now time to leave the notion of learning behind and follow Mintzberg's trail into the world of overt and, at times, covert influence.

Power and politics

The power school appeals to those of us who believe that influence and politics are at the heart of strategic management. Here the shareholder interests are brought into conflict with those of a wider set of stakeholders. These stakeholders being represented as the target or real driver behind strategy making. The process of strategy formulation and execution then becomes one of trying to balance or manipulate the demands of the stakeholders with the desires and limitations of those in power. The challenge is usually around how to share scarce resources while at the same time dealing with a changing environment, perceptions of risk, and competitors' actions. From the macro level or external perspective the power school has given us the notion of strategy making that relies on co-operation between firms. Here we have the whole raft of joint ventures, alliances, franchising, licensing, outsourcing and supply chain management. The suggestion here is that organizations are forced into setting up informal and formal networks to pursue effective power strategies.

Culture

The core idea here is that every organization has a set of shared beliefs that characterize the organization for the inmates and that these shared beliefs provide management and staff with a sense of stability. Terms such as "cultural web" and "organizational paradigm" are employed to capture this notion of how individuals socialize and establish an implicit set of rules as to how the business activities and strategies are to be played out. This idea – that a unified set of beliefs exists that drives interpretation and action – has obvious implications for how the business development process is managed. If the culture is sufficiently homogeneous and focused then it can either be a help or block to development and change. The current popularity attached to the idea of managing change programs by manipulating the dominant culture so that it aligns with the desired business direction, shows how deeply this notion has become ingrained in the management rule book.

Environment

Here the strategist is caricatured as a passive victim of forces external to the organization, doomed to waiting for events to unfold and then attempting to react and sustain a state of temporary survival. Proponents of this school see the organizational response being to adapt to these environmental pressures or die. The analogy of a sailing ship in a storm captures this notion quite well. Researchers have attempted to identify these pressures and in doing so provide much needed guidance to the organizational strategists. Mintzberg has suggested that there are four key dimensions that will help us to understand these environmental pressures:

- the degree of stability (the uncertainty that surrounds features in the environment)

- the perception of complexity (the extent to which the knowledge required to run the business, is perceived as sophisticated)

- the diversity of the firm's market offerings (where multiple products and services are applied to multiple markets)

- the hostility (the extent to which the competition, external groups and access to resources impact on strategy making).

We are also advised that the strategist is pressurized and constrained by industry regulation, the constant threat of imitation from competitors and the resistance to change created by the build up of expert knowledge within the organization. No wonder that this school has such a large following. The main criticism is that environments are created by the decisions and actions of managers within the businesses. Hence these environmental pressures may simply represent perceptions based on rationalizations that follow from action taking. Their reality being a mental construct resulting from action rather than from having an objective reality.

> The strategist is pressurized and constrained by industry regulation, the constant threat of imitation from competitors and the resistance to change created by the build up of expert knowledge within the organization

Configuration

This school of thought promotes the view that the business development process is focused on matching the organizational structure to the business context. Also that the organization exhibits various stages of growth as the environment and the capabilities of the organization change. The notion that both the industry and the organization have life cycles is used by this school. Moves between the stages in the life cycle are then argued to be dictating the extent and timing of strategies that are required to transform the organization. In some organizations and contexts the change to strategies will be incremental, in others much more radical. If there is one key message from this school, it is that organizational structures have to adapt as the strategies change.

Faced with such a battery of perspectives we are literally spoilt for choice. The academics will argue that their perspective is the one to believe, while the management consultants will offer a much more sugar coated pill. The reality is that we select the perspective that matches our level of credulity and has proven useful in the past. For example, when faced with an audience that expects to see a definitive and clear set of strategies the temptation is to draw on the prescriptive approaches. These conventional approaches to developing and implementing strategies for business growth have popular appeal. They are at the foundation of all strategic management courses and the approaches used by many management consultants. It is only when these clearly defined approaches fail to produce results that, like Merlin, we reach further into our book for explanations and spells. The challenge of strategic thinking will always be how to make sense of uncertainty and ambiguity when facing complex business situations. The management gurus and theorists have provided us with some pointers, or at least a broad framework on which to build our personal strategy. We now need to see how this advice has been taken up by managers and where it has resulted in success.

> The challenge of strategic thinking will always be how to make sense of uncertainty and ambiguity when facing complex business situations

What can successful companies tell us?

In business we will find many examples of the art of compromise in action. Rather than getting hung up over whether business success depends on detailed planning and analysis or just emerges, most managers accept that it is probably a bit of both. They quickly learn how to change a business idea or decision that fails to deliver. Making a business idea work in the marketplace, knowing how far to stretch the desire for growth and how to continually move from one business plateau to the next is the hallmark of an adaptable organization. The management of this planning with adhocracy paradox can best be demonstrated by looking at how The Walt Disney Company and Compaq have learned to adapt.

Walt Disney

When Walt Disney died in 1966 the company went through a period of rapid decline. The culture that had developed was one where innovation and proposals for change from within the management had not been encouraged. An approach that relied on living off the brand name could no longer sustain growth. The theme park business was in decline, with attendance falling, and even the opening of the Epcot center at Orlando and Disneyland in Tokyo failed to maintain revenues. Revenue from the film business and video sales had also declined in the face of strong competition from the major studios and very few new releases were being made.

The appointment of Michael Eisner in 1984 signalled the start of a turnaround strategy. Over the next two years he added new attractions to the theme parks and raised entry fees by 50 per cent, re-released original Disney favourite films as videos, generated a whole new range of animated films and finally launched the new Disney Stores chain.

Here we see an example of a planned but at the same time, adaptive, approach to developing strategies to grow a business. The approach was to build all three businesses while at the same time creating linkages and synergies.

In the next four years Disney's sales had increased from $1.66 billion to $3.75 billion and net profits from $98 million to $570 million, and its stock market valuation from $1.8 billion to $10.3 billion. The basis of this outstanding success was an ability to link brand name with capabilities that included a massive film archive and know-how in animation, while balancing experimentation with the need for focus. The original film making had given rise to television shows and the creation of Disneyland. Disneyland was allowed to develop into two businesses:

- Epcot, Tokyo, Euro Disney, Animal Kingdom and then full blown theme parks
- hotels, planned communities, cruise liners and vacation resorts.

The television business expanded into dedicated channel broadcasting, live theater shows and filmed entertainment.

The early licensing of the film characters had, over the years, led to music and book publishing. This formed the basis for Eisner's move into setting up Disney Stores. He started with a prototype in Glendale, California in 1987, which enabled some 700 stores to be established in the USA and across the world by 1996. These stores sold thousands of different licensed products and created links to the other business activities and brands.

One of the keys to the success of this strategy was the willingness of the business managers to experiment, while at the same time being able to decide when the business idea should be fixed. By fixing the business idea at the point where there was sufficient visibility and clear indications of profitability, Disney Stores could then be expanded by following well tested business approaches. The executive management had confidence in their profit expectations and knew the precise level of investment required. This ability to switch from a planned strategy to experimentation and then back to a planned strategy is the key to the success at Disney World. They have taken advantage of the planning with adhocracy paradox presented by our gurus and theorists.

Compaq

At Compaq the dilemma was how to adapt in the face of a severe challenge to what had been a period of meteoric growth.

Compaq had been founded in 1983 by Rod Cannion who, with a small team of engineers, had used Intel's 386 CPU to produce a viable competitor in the IBM compatible PC market. Then in late 1990 the market was flooded with cheap clones that eroded Compaq's market share. Compaq had followed a differentiation strategy, enabling them to produce high end PCs based on the latest technology and charge high prices to business users. They relied on a specialized dealer network to distribute and support the product. Their investment in research and development, coupled with a culture that valued quality, meant that they were unable to respond to these low cost clones. As in similar cases of this kind, a new Chief Executive, Echard Pfeiffer, was appointed to revitalize the company fortunes. Once again a familiar initial formula for recovery followed: cuts to the workforce, smaller management overheads and dealer margins. By 1994 the company was back into profitability and was the world's leading PC company. Pfeiffer's approach relied on pursuing four strategies:

- becoming a lead player in the low cost PC market
- focusing on cost reduction in manufacturing and distribution thus improving profitability and enabling competitors' prices to be matched
- accelerating the rate of new product development
- expanding the product range and functions.

Changing the distribution strategy from specialized dealers to mail order, enabled Compaq to compete directly with companies such as Dell and AST. Compaq offered next day delivery, home installation and long warranties. Having ensured that the company could compete with low entry cost newcomers, Pfeiffer then began to segment the market and design and launch notebooks, low end business PCs, professional workstations and large servers.

Compaq's markets are now global, extending to Europe, Japan, South America and the Asia Pacific region.

These two companies give us a good insight into how theory is rapidly integrated and used in practice. But before moving on to look more closely at what appears to have been almost second nature to these management teams, we need to look at one more example of theory in action. Nokia, the cellular telephone company, shows us how a company can change its strategy game play from one of acquisition and mergers to one where technological excellence dominates, to one of consumer product marketing.

Nokia

Nokia was founded over one hundred years ago, in Finland, as a pulp and paper manufacturer. Over the years the company had diversified into a wide range of businesses. In the 1980s it was seen as a conglomerate with businesses as diverse as rubber tire manufacturing, paper products manufacturing, consumer electronics and telecommunications. Today Nokia is one of the world leaders in the manufacture of mobile phones, wireless communications and global satellite-based digital cellular communications systems. It has a turnover of some $12 billion, with sales and earnings growing at some 25 per cent per annum.

In the 1980s the new CEO, Kari Kairamo, held the vision that Nokia could become a global corporation by adopting an acquisition, merger and joint venture strategy. The company made 21 acquisitions between 1986 and 1989, eventually owning a very diverse set of businesses. Sales grew but the earnings fell, a familiar story where this type of unfocused growth through acquisition strategy is followed. Acquisitions are often made at a cost that is often not recouped. In 1989 the net losses were over $50 million. The suggested causes ranged from increased competition in the consumer electronics market, losses in traditional low-growth businesses, an inability to gain the synergies anticipated from the acquisitions, the world economy downturn and failure to safeguard contracts made with the Soviet Union. The tragic death of Kairamo in December 1988 was followed by the appointment of a new president, Simo Vuorilehto.

Over the years Nokia had, along with a string of unrelated companies, also acquired a unique bundle of capabilities. The climatic conditions in Finland made it prohibitively expensive to lay down traditional wire line telephone services. The provision of cellular telephones thus became imperative for countries such as Sweden and Norway as well as Finland. In 1994 some 12 per cent of Scandinavians owned cellular phones compared to the USA's 6 per cent. Another feature that had helped Nokia develop a capability for low cost development and production was that in Finland there had been no national telephone service, and hence the market was supplied by over 50 autonomous companies. Low cost provision was the key to survival within Finland and would form the basis for competitive advantage outside.

In 1992 a new CEO, Jorma Ollila, set out to introduce a strategy that focused on the telecommunications sector and non core businesses were sold off. The company had moved from growth by acquisition to one that focused on becoming the world leader in digital cellular technology provision. Partnerships were formed with technology leaders across the world to support this strategy. Nokia also changed its market focus from the high margin/high volume business user to a wider set of customers. Following the example set by Motorola it now offers devices in a range of colors and styles, creating a blend between a high technology product and fashion setting.

Learning to market, distribute and provide support to this new set of users is the current challenge facing Nokia. With revenues of $11.4 billion in 1997 and a presence in over 40 countries, Nokia has clearly demonstrated that creating and protecting a unique set of capabilities while encouraging an adaptable approach to strategy is the key to long-term success.

These three examples have demonstrated that there is no real gap between the theory and practice in business development. This should be no surprise. The stories and rationalizations as to what was intended and what transpired are researched and reported by authors who are using a common language. Our CEOs have also been exposed to this language and to the associated set of concepts as to how businesses should be developed and what to do when faced with a complex situation. There will obviously be variations in the particular circumstances that executives face. Personal interpretations based on deeply held values and beliefs will lead to different actions. There are some common messages to be gained from the three examples presented above.

- First, that formerly successful companies are overtaken by events that they either failed to anticipate, or saw and decided to ignore.
- Second, that companies need to concentrate on maintaining the current wealth-creating business idea while at the same time building the next one.
- Third, that the ability to adapt planned strategies and recognize the value of unplanned ones that emerge is a key capability that must be developed and become an ingrained approach.

SUMMARY

This Part 1 introduced the notion that when engaged in business development we are playing a game against other players. The Nelson Hind case study provided an opportunity to identify your preferred approach to playing the business development game. This may have given you a few surprises or perhaps provided a welcome boost to your confidence as a player. We then looked at some of the rules of the game, identifying the pure game theory approach adopted by the chess players and the devotees of the algorithm while not forgetting the behavioralists who suggest that rationalization and self serving motivations reduce the value of *knowing the rules*. As the number of players increases then the complexity of the game obviously accelerates. When faced with many players we saw that the conventional approach to competition was to adopt the notion of positioning in the marketplace and providing customers with added value. In these situations, businesses are arguably under the constant threat of their products and services being copied or substitutes being found by both competitors and customers. But the ultimate challenge to a business is where a new way of understanding and playing the game is developed and introduced by a newcomer or one of the players.

We then looked at how the perspectives held by key players affect their motivation and approach to the game. We were able to take comfort from contemporary research into the behaviors of key business leaders which shows that it is possible to detect recurring patterns and styles being used. The styles varied according to the role that the parent or power group adopt in their quest for business growth. Understanding the structure and the history of a business can also provide a good insight into why the game is being played in a particular way. A review of the core beliefs and behaviors of the strategists enabled us to draw on Henry Mintzberg's work of categorizing the various schools of thought. This will help to set the scene for later stages in the book by revealing how the prescriptive approach has come to dominate the way strategy is promoted in business schools. Ways that have now been internalized by many leading businesses and their managers. It is only where these approaches have failed to deliver results that other explanations such as learning, entrepreneurism, and power and politics have gained support.

The academics and gurus continue to argue for the best way to understand and play the competitive business game. But none of the arguments seem to adequately address the problems that arise when businesses attempt to apply the espoused wisdom. We gained some inspiration from examples of business development in action from the efforts of companies such as Walt Disney, Compaq and Nokia. Perhaps the efforts of the gurus and researchers have not all been in vain. The strategists and CEOs in these companies had all been exposed to the gurus and their theories and it is perhaps no surprise that they then rationalize and explain their behaviors using the language of the business schools.

In Part 2 we take a hard look at how businesses seek an approach or logic that will beat the competition. Your success in creating an effective operation and developing a sustainable competitive business proposition depends on acquiring a superior approach. There are lessons to be learned from the experts and from businesses and we need to put this under the microscope. This will put our quest to develop an overarching and personal business strategy into context with current business thinking. The next step is to discover what has to be learned in order to become a better strategist.

Part **2**

Becoming a
better strategist

Chapter **3**

The quest for a business logic

Rules and models destroy genius and art

William Hazlitt (1778–1830), British Essayist

Identifying your business approach

We find comfort in the belief that our thinking and actions have an underlying logic, that our actions are defensible and have an explicable consistency. Once we can understand and explain the logic behind our thinking then we get the feeling that all is well. We take it for granted that managers in other businesses are also searching for a logic that will enable them to play the game with greater panache and dash than their competitors.

As an experienced manager you will have already developed your own approach to dealing with the complexity involved in business situations. The business scenario provided below gives you an opportunity to check out your approach. Your task is to read the case and then answer the questions that I have posed. Allow about 20 minutes for the reading and then 10 minutes to answer the questions. Here I am looking for a reasonably quick response in order to bring out the ingrained approach that you use to find patterns in and make sense of a business situation.

Recipes for a healthier brand image

Any business that is involved in organic food ought to be a sure-fire winner. The British market may be small – organic food accounts for only 2 per cent of grocery sales – but it is growing rapidly. Sales have increased more than tenfold in recent years to about £1 billion a year, according to industry estimates. The furore over genetically modified food can only boost them further.

It was this phenomenal growth that prompted a group of young London entrepreneurs to acquire the troubled organic food company Whole Earth earlier this year for £2.5 million. They are led by William Kendall, the man who revived the

New Covent Garden Soup Company, and include Henry Tinsley, whose family company Tinsley Foods makes chilled meals and sandwiches for the big retail chains.

"Whole Earth is a fantastic brand," says Kendall. "It is the original diversified organic brand. There are now rivals in each of our main product groups but there is nobody who embraces the range in the way that we do."

But that range of products has not led to profitability in recent years. The company was started 30 years ago by the American-born Craig Sams and it appears to be stuck in a time warp. Growing numbers of the British public may be shunning food produced by industrial farming methods, let alone genetically modified food, but the converts to organic food, essentially middle-class urbanites, also crave a degree of sophistication. A recent focus group revealed that the Whole Earth image was more synonymous with ageing hippies and brown rice than fettucini and organic rocket.

Whole Earth's products are on the shelves of all Britain's big supermarket chains but face growing competition from rivals whose peanut butters, spreads and cereals often appear more desirable and better packaged. Small organic companies such as Jordan's and Dove Farm, which make cereals, or St Dalfour, which makes spreads and jams, are finding no difficulty in accessing the supermarkets. In addition, Whole Earth is having to contend with the supermarket's own-label organic brands.

By the time Kendall and his investors took over the company, Whole Earth was in a precarious state. Sales had been growing steadily to £7 million a year but the company was losing money. "We found a company with all these products," says Kendall, "some of them successful and very popular, but losing money and going bust." Most of the £2.5 million put up by Kendall and his backers to acquire 80 per cent of the company has been used to reduce its debts. This leaves a modest budget for re-marketing the brand, which will make life tough for Kendall and his new management team. They must modernize the company's image without the resources enjoyed by larger rivals for the makeovers and advertising. At the same time. they must also try to remain true to the company's roots; to exploit the company's traditional commitment to ethical organic food production. The company must also establish proper management systems, as well as cut back on some of its product lines and the number of manufacturers it uses.

Despite the problems, Whole Earth has some real gems. One of them is the Green and Black organic chocolate range launched by Sams' wife, the consumer affairs journalist Jo Farley. Run as a separate brand under the Whole Earth company, Green and Black has cornered about 90 per cent of the market for organic chocolate. But there are other areas where the company's track record has not been so impressive. One of its problems has been the lack of management control, something that afflicts many small companies and can prove fatal for one with a turnover as large as Whole Earth's. The company has produced regular audited accounts, but its happy clappy approach to management meant that the information needed to take proper decisions was often lacking. Moreover, Sams' campaigning role in promoting the organic movement tended to distract him from day-to-day running of the business.

As with companies such as Virgin, which are essentially marketing groups for their own brands, Whole Earth has no manufacturing facilities of its own. Based in London's Portobello Road, it gets a variety of manufacturers to make up products to its own specification. But in Whole Earth's case this has led to a lack of discipline, with both product range and the number of manufacturers used proliferating. The company has more than 100 product lines, and at one stage had 200. Further pruning is likely, with products such as tinned brown rice likely to disappear. There are obvious cost advantages in not owning your own manufacturing site, but this encouraged Whole Earth to be profligate. The boundless enthusiasm for all things organic encouraged Sams to launch endless new ranges, without sufficient marketing clout to support them. Had the company had its own manufacturing facilities, like the New Covent Garden Soup Company, for example, the sheer cost of production would have quickly forced it to focus on the more successful lines.

"Part of the problem has been the attitude that our products are produced with love," says Kendall. "They have to be produced by the right people using all the right products. That makes it emotionally difficult to get rid of these lines if they fail. But if they do, we will need to kill them. What we need is fewer products that we can give better support to." The proliferation of Whole Earth's range is already imposing a strain on the company's resources. Just dealing with the big supermarkets sometimes involves the company visiting the cereal buyer, the ice cream buyer, the jam buyer, the pasta buyer and so on. Yet at present the company has only one full-time sales representative who has to visit the big five chains as well as all the independent outlets. This leaves little time to address the fast expanding food-service companies – the host of cappuccino and sandwich bars, the corporate canteens – that are springing up all over the country and which Kendall would like Whole Earth to target. As part of its efforts to build up the sales and marketing strength, the company is moving to more modern premises later in the year near London's Waterloo station. These will offer not only modern kitchen facilities but will also house the expanded management team, which will rise to about 20 in the next few months.

Much of the new management's time has been spent on pondering how Whole Earth's dated image can be overhauled. "When we took over the company," says Kendall, "my in-tray was brimming over with proposals from designers and image consultants." Caroline Jeremy, the new creative force behind the New Covent

Garden Soup Company, and now installed as Whole Earth's marketing director, took the soup manufacturer's cartons through several evolutionary updates without any radical changes of image. But in Whole Earth's case the company must leap almost 30 years, with all the dangers that entails. Those creative skills will be tested to the hilt when the company launches its own cola drink in the autumn. Whole Earth will be promoting its healthy qualities. The drink is said to have a restorative effect, gently lifting energy levels rather than delivering the sudden rush that is common with some fizzy drinks. It is also kinder to the teeth because it lacks phosphoric acid. And it is made from real cola beans. Kendall and Jeremy believe the product will represent a decisive move away from Whole Earth's staid image. They are also confident that the meager marketing budget will not hamper the new product's success. Again, the Covent Garden Soup Company is the role model. "When we started making our fresh soup, we really had to fight to persuade the supermarkets to take it. When they did, it suddenly took off without any marketing budget," says Kendall. As it does not have money to splash around, Whole Earth will adopt what Kendall calls "guerilla marketing" tactics. "It is about looking for opportunities. It's about public relations, doing tastings and going to the right food shows. It's about persuading key consumers to believe that this is their brand so that they will tell their friends about us. Ben and Jerry did it with ice cream and so did we at the soup company." The larger than life do-gooding image of Ben and Jerry played a big part in that company's success.

Sams and his family have retained a 20 per cent holding in Whole Earth, a situation that could lead to conflict in the company. But Kendall believes the position is a positive one. Sams' new role will allow him to do what he has always done best. He will champion the organic cause and use his well-established skills to locate rare organic produce and to help the company's manufacturers to conform to organic standards of production. His presence will also ensure that the company's traditional strengths remain in place. Whole Earth's association with ethical issues, and its involvement with the Fairtrade Foundation, is something that consumers increasingly insist on and could become a powerful tool in the company's marketing strategy. According to Kendall, Whole Earth has always been a company of "enormous aspirations." But if those aspirations are to be met and Whole Earth is to profit from the upswing in organic food, much work remains to be done.

Acknowledgements: *The Sunday Times*, August 29, 1999.
Jane Renton, The Enterprise Network. Copyright Times Newspapers Limited.

TASK

Assume that you have accepted the job of Chief Executive at Whole Earth and that you have a contract that includes a substantial annual bonus related to bottom line performance improvements. You will also acquire a 10 per cent share in the business, to be awarded at the end of two years, if, in that time, you double the turnover while maintaining bottom line performance at the industry average. Show on the following grid your initial thoughts about how to make a success of the job. You should make one "tick" for each of the propositions.

Figure 3.1 Identifying your business approach

	Strongly support			No view			Strongly against	
Propositions about how to make a success of your job at Whole Earth	+3	+2	+1	0	−1	−2	−3	Total
1 My starting point will be to set financial targets.								
2 Collecting market share data and information on competitor profiles is a priority.								
3 I must obtain figures on contribution made by product then cut back.								
4 It is essential that clear objectives for growth in sales for each product are established and met.								
5 Costs must be contained and suppliers squeezed.								
6 Key customers must be identified and their loyalty won over.								
7 The company management systems must be tightened up.								
8 The sales function will be outsourced.								
9 The Cola launch must be planned to the last detail.								
10 Sams must be controlled and directed.								
11 We need to establish a vision and a detailed strategic plan for growing the company.								
12 Identifying the industry value chains and where we can add value to the company value chain is a priority.								
13 I will establish a culture that promotes creativity.								
14 Promotion of our image as an ethical company is key to our success.								
15 The funding for media promotion of our company is vital.								
16 I want to see our key products being linked in a campaign that promotes healthy but exciting living.								

Your answers will have been based on ingrained approaches that you use to understand and manage complex business situations. These approaches are made up from the following elements.

1. A desire to discover the rules of the game and the context in which it is being played. (Questions 1, 2, 3 and 4)

2. The level of confidence that you have in your ability to play and control the game. (Questions 5, 6, 7 and 8)

3. The extent to which you rely on formal logic, past winning plays or on intuition. (Questions 9, 10, 11 and 12)

4. How you evaluate the risks involved and use creative approaches. (Questions 13, 14, 15 and 16)

Add up your total scores for questions 1 to 4, 5 to 8, 9 to 12 and 13 to 16 and then see how your business logic shows itself.

Discovering the rules of the game and context (questions 1–4)

A high positive score indicates that you have digested a great deal of theory about business development or have been exposed to ideas from marketing and other functional disciplines. You like to have a clear picture of the business issues being faced and are prepared to make some early judgements about how complex these issues really are. Your experience in business has given you a high degree of confidence in conventional management theory. You are prepared to use it to understand a business issue and have had some successes. You find that using a conventional approach, with its clear methods and explanations, enables you to instil confidence among your colleagues. It gives them a clear picture of your intentions and actions.

A high negative score will confirm that you either have had some bad experiences, or failures, associated with using conventional theories and approaches. It could also tell you that your belief in such theories being of any practical use is minimal.

Confidence in playing and controlling the game (questions 5–8)

A high positive score indicates that you look at a company from an industry level viewpoint. Your favored approach is to categorize the key issues facing the company into those that are short term and straightforward and those full of uncertainty and ambiguity. You like to see how big a gap there is between current and desired performance and what has to be done to close the gap. In your view the industry setting, including structural features and competitors' actions, will dictate and determine what can and has to be done. You like to identify the critical success factors in an industry as a precursor to specifying the choices that have to be made and hence the strategic decisions.

A high negative score suggests that you see all business situations as requiring the same approach. You may well be very experienced and confident in your ability to make decisions and then force them through to action. The perspective that you adopt is that of driving the company from a keen insight into its key capabilities and then taking on the outside world as events arise. It is also likely that you are happy to change the outside world to suit the business game that you want to be playing.

Reliance on formal logic, past plays or intuition (questions 9–12)

A high positive score suggests that you are a master of logical argument. You make use of major premises and conclusive statements, as a way of convincing yourself and others that you have made sense of a situation. You rely on gathering data or evidence in a logical fashion, using techniques that are readily recognized and accepted by your colleagues. For example, you would rely on financial data, market data, customer surveys, and competitor profiling to generate the information from which your logic can be spelt out.

A high negative score suggests that you use intuition to make sense of a situation. Some would say that you "fly by the seat of your pants." You are either used to having your own way or make use of political power, lobbying and informal social networks to influence others. You may have little or no faith in analysis or have found by experience that intuitive approaches are easier to implement. Being able to influence others through argument and the use of your imagination is an approach that you have perfected.

How you evaluate risks involved and use creative approaches (questions 13–16)

A high positive score marks you out as an entrepreneur. You operate best in situations where you have a lot of experience of both the markets and the technology and where your skills can run unchecked. You would not make a good "number two." You look for the risk in situations as a source of opportunity rather than as a problem to be resolved. Faced with a complex set of issues you rely on the use of intuition, either your own or your colleagues'. Finding creative and break-out approaches is high on your agenda and drives your thinking.

A high negative score suggests that you have worked in industries with a very long life cycle. Change and uncertainty have not featured highly in your experiences and you are used to following a low risk approach in complex situations. Intuition is something that you prefer to use in private settings and find it difficult to talk openly with colleagues about the more inspirational thoughts that might come into your subconsciousness. You are probably a safe pair of hands and liked by those who want to see a steady, low-risk return for their investment.

Finding the best approach

If there exists a universal logic that once discovered and applied would enable a firm to generate profits above the average for the industry, then imitation by competitors would, over time, erode away that advantage. The proverbial bar would be raised for all firms. In spite of this apparently fatalistic view, the gurus and consultants earn an alleged $15 billion each year advising firms how to find such a logic or how to get back on to the shining path. Perhaps they are in the business of raising the bar each year so that the next wave of managers has to compete just that much harder. A failed guru would no doubt argue that their advice was sound but it had been misinterpreted and our old foe "bad luck" just seemed to ruin the day. The consulting industry is in itself competitive. They too are seeking the winning logic. The struggle has taken them from business process re-engineering, to competitive positioning, to core competences, to stakeholder value, to learning organizations, and now knowledge management. The consultants and gurus are also scrambling to adjust their advice and approaches to incorporate the growth of e-business and the coming of age of the internet. But the gurus never give up, they tell us that all is not lost.

They admit that the performance of a business is the result of many forces and events and that many of these are random and totally unpredictable. But they argue that where a logic is found and followed, then that prescription will affect performance of the firm over a long period. That even in situations that are apparently chaotic there is a long-term pattern. The point that they make is that there may be no "rules for riches" but there are general rules for "improving chance for riches." This advice suggests that there is a way of almost guessing at the path to follow. Business leaders are encouraged to believe that applying a broad logic will influence the chance of generating above average profits. This whole area is based on the notion that there is a strong causal relationship between setting people goals and achieving superior business performance. An approach that is argued to work even when the business executive is faced with a wide range of approaches from which to choose. The mere act of setting goals, no matter how certain we are that they are achievable, will inspire managers to take action and seek ways of achieving them.

> Business leaders are encouraged to believe that applying a broad logic will influence the chance of generating above average profits

Here the gurus are telling us something that we would on face value take for granted. They argue that if the path to achieving a position of competitive advantage involves reacting to a random series of events, then the winners are more likely to be those that have freedom to choose how to react. Encouraging managers to make local decisions would sound like good advice, but choice assumes three things:

- one, that the managers have the best available information;
- two, that they are equipped to make these choices; and
- three, that they will make decisions that are in the best interests of the stakeholders.

Quite a set of assumptions and an incredible demand on the business manager who, in most businesses, is in effect a "hired hand." So if we are arguing that there are no clear prescriptions or approaches that will enable us to win the business game, then why is it that anyone would even contemplate accepting a prescription for success? Managers would just settle for doing the best they can and try to cope with the reactions of managers in other businesses who are doing the same thing. Adopting strategies that made the best of a bad job and gave the opposition the worst of what they had would be seen as a good strategy. Fortunately it is not as demoralizing as this and most firms now recognize that there is value to be gained from co-operation as well as competition. A glance at the business press will quickly confirm how the alliances, acquisitions and mergers approach has gained favour among previously isolationist-minded managers.

In the absence of any deterministic rules, we find that the best advice from the gurus boils down to a formula that says "do the best that you can in the circumstances." But businesses and the thousands of managers who now drive industry and commerce have taken the notion of managerialism to heart, adhering to a belief system that tells us to set clear goals and manage our way towards them. Advising people that eating an elephant becomes feasible once you use a small spoon may not be politically correct, but for most managers it is what they do every day. We need to have a long-term view while at the same time focusing on managing the here and now. Two leading consultants, Gary Hamel and Keith Prahalad, have captured this notion with the expression strategic intent.

Strategic intent comes from top management and by virtue of the long-term stability it provides, middle management are able to concentrate on the more medium-term business activities. The outcomes or goals for the firm are aimed clearly at gaining competitive advantage. The means of achieving this are seen as emerging and flexing as circumstances change and the learning grows. Hamel and Prahalad recognize this problem of facing the realities of needing to run and sustain an existing business, while at the same time pursuing longer-term strategies and aspirations.

66We believe that it is essential for top management to set out an aspiration that creates, by design, a chasm between ambition and resources. An explicit emphasis on the notion of 'fit,' and the way in which the idea of fit is embedded in strategy tools often deflects managers from the enormously important task of creating a misfit between resources and ambitions. Of course, at any one time there must be a loose fit between short-term objectives and the near-at-hand resources. But even then the fit should not be too tight. 99

Hamel, G. and Prahalad, C.K. (1994) Competing for the Future.

Clarifying and declaring the strategic intent, capturing and sharing a vision for the business, and "doing our best" are all sound notions. But they are too conceptual to be of real use in helping to identify business options and make decisions over how to allocate scarce resources. Business managers at the General Electric Company tackled this concern over 40 years ago with a landmark project that adopted the acronym PIMS (Profit Impact of Marketing Strategy). We need to see what they were trying to do, and ask: "Did it work?" and "Does it give us the approach or logic that we are looking for?"

GEC

The idea behind PIMS was that given sufficient evidence from a large number of businesses in a variety of situations, links between strategies and business performance could be found. The model could then be used to make predictions about likely outcomes of any proposed strategizing. A model that relied on the notion of regression was to be developed that would explain the variations that were being experienced in returns made from investments. Finding the key variables and their impact on the returns was the goal sought by the GE gurus. Prestigious institutions such as Harvard Business School, the Marketing Science Institute, the Strategic Planning Institute and over 200 companies from a wide range of industries all contributed to developing and validating the processes and outputs from this "once and for all" approach to identifying a business logic.

Some excellent and searching questions were being asked of this model. Such as:

- What causes the variations in cash flows and returns on investment among similar businesses?
- If a known strategy is applied in a known set of market conditions in a known industry, then what returns and cash flows can be expected?

As in all models the validity of the outcomes depends on not only the accuracy of the input data and the relationships that have been built in, but also on the definitions given to the variables. In the PIMS model 37 variables were included, such as: product quality, market share, market growth rate, investment levels, etc. The modellers argued that there are generic rules that apply to markets in all industries and geographic locations and hence any cries that "my business is unique" could be argued or explained away. The five variables that the PIMS model highlighted as most important in influencing the likely performance of a firm were:

- attractiveness of the market (growth rate and stage in the product or service life cycle)

- competitive position (market share, relative product/service quality and the breadth of the product/service portfolio)

- how effectively investments were being used (capital to sales and value added to sales ratios, utilization of capacity)

- flexibility in budget allocations (marketing expenses to sales, research and development expenses to sales, new product expenses to sales ratios)

- changes in market share.

Runs of the model showed that the major variables that impacted on return on investment were:

- intensity of investment
- relative market share
- market growth rate
- stage in the product or service life cycle
- marketing expenses to sales ratio.

The results of the PIMS studies

This all sounds fairly obvious to us now and this is because the prescriptions from the PIMS work have, over the past 40 years, been embedded into the minds of thousands of managers. The prescription that resulted from the PIMS studies are usually expressed in the form of a major premise statement with sub-premises. The business arguments are almost totally reliant on using logic to reach an indisputable conclusion. But the presence of so many uncertainties and ambiguities results in the argument being aimed at persuasion and demonstrating conviction. A typical premise statement on how to ensure a return on investment greater than the industry average using the PIMS advice, could be stated as follows:

Success will follow from our ability to attract and commit to the levels of investment necessary to sustain our technological lead and having the capacity available to seize expansion opportunities presented by our growing markets. By selecting and competing in high growth markets with a portfolio of products and services that embrace the embryonic to the mature we will be able to maintain and increase our operating margins. Our sales will grow as a result of our pursuit of a market positioning strategy that depends on investments in brand image and maintaining customer loyalty. We must be vigilant and responsive to the changing needs of our existing and potential customers.

It sounds familiar and very persuasive. Finding holes in the logic is not easy and to argue against such an oration would appear to be churlish if not downright disloyal. As with all prescriptions the value is both in understanding the devil in the detail and getting the balance right. For example, as investment increases there will be a time lag before the increased market share allows some premium prices to be charged or until the economies of scale benefits can be realized, an argument that is used by all e-business start ups and some of the more established ones such as Amazon.com. As everyone who has tried to grow a business knows, it is the temporal effects, the impact of unpredictable events, and the actions of competitors that call for skills beyond those of a rule follower. But, to be fair, the PIMS gurus did state that the model was dependent on probabilities and that the prescriptions only showed the extent to which confidence could be placed on the impact of pursuing a particular approach. They stressed that the model was only an aid and that business success still depended on the judgement of the business managers.

During the past 40 years views and beliefs about how to develop businesses have changed enormously. The prevailing approach that still dominates management thinking, is where strategies are driven down from the top and controls applied that ensure their implementation goes to plan. An approach that works in relatively stable industry contexts. At the same time, in industries where there is rapid change, intense global competition and the need for business decisions to be taken at operational levels, new approaches to strategic management have been developed. These developments have taken managers beyond the determinism suggested by the PIMS. But PIMS and the era of the top-down strategic planners has had such an impact on the beliefs associated with prescriptions for business growth that it deserves our attention. In the next section we will see what the more contemporary approaches to modelling business have produced.

Is it all about having a superior business model?

If we start by assuming that a winning business logic exists then we are also assuming that this logic, if followed, will produce outcomes that will satisfy the owners or stockholders. Outcomes such as: growth of the stock price, a high price to earnings ratio, financial market premiums (the ratio of the value of all the financial claims on a firm, including stocks and bonds, to the replacement value of the firm's assets) and accounting profitability (the ratio of the after tax value of the income to the book value of the assets). These will all influence whether investors will buy, hold or sell the stock. Their decisions will be also be based on perceptions of the potential benefits rather than on some guaranteed measure. We would also want the logic to be "generalizable" so that we did not have to find a new logic for every circumstance.

All the research to date tells us that we are out of luck – that there is no universal logic – but in its place there are tools of analysis and models that get us closer to understanding what happens when businesses attempt to play the game. These analytical tools have been developed by the economists and the financiers who are fascinated with measures of output and less interested in the decision-making processes that are involved. Here we have a host of models developed by researchers such as Michael Porter who focused on producing guidance or rules for creating sustainable competitive advantage. The empiricists on the other hand prefer to tap into large databases of evidence to glean some indication of the relationships between key features of an industry and results of decisions that managers have made.

Although these attempts to provide a clear business logic have failed, they do give some guidance on how to manage the business opportunities and challenges that are ahead. If we cannot expect to be given a business logic then perhaps we can look for guidance in the form of what have been described as "well tested business models," learning from the approaches that have been used by the small as well as the great and the good to continue to achieve high performance in their industries.

The McGahan study

The performance of publicly traded US firms has been compiled since 1980 and is available in the Compustat Business Segment Reports. This data has been used by researchers Anita McGahan and Michael Porter in a number of studies aimed at identifying fundamental facts about business performance in various economic sectors. A recent report by Anita McGahan (1999) described in the *California Management Review*, 41(3) gives us an excellent insight into the attempts made by businesses to find a winning business logic or model. More importantly it highlights the existence of an underlying pattern or logic to their efforts. This survey covered the period 1981 to 1997 and included over 13,000 business segments in around 8,000 corporations representing over 650 industries. A massive data set from which we would expect to be able to detect and capture winning business approaches and logic.

The Gannet Corporation

One business that stands out in McGahan's report in terms of having sustained a high level of performance over the period, is the Gannet Corporation: average profitability around 26 per cent with assets of some $2.2 billion, an average revenue growth of 8.4 per cent and an average financial market premium of 1.91. Gannet are in the newspaper business, publishing *USA Today* and some 80 local newspapers with daily and weekly circulation. It is seen to be in an attractive industry and is part of a high performing corporate parent. In the late 1980s and early 1990s Gannet are reported as operating in three industries that covered news broadcasting, outdoor advertising and newspaper publishing. Over the period, Gannet's performance was above average for these industries and this has been partly ascribed to the effective corporate management of the divisions. The principal competitors adopted quite different marketing and distribution strategies. For example, the *Wall Street Journal* concentrated on business news, the *Washington Post* on political reporting and the *New York Times* on national news and popular features.

Anita McGahan suggests that the high industry level performance was possible due to the broad differentiation among the leading competitors. This is an example of an industry where there are wide variations in the dominant business idea and business logic used by the main competitors. Gannet focused on publication of local newspapers. The editorial control was decentralized but the coverage of national and world news was centralized. The printing system was distributed, which guaranteed cost efficiency and timely physical distribution. McGahan suggests that success was due to management being able to sustain high profitability within the industry without destroying the industry structure. Obviously such a high performance attracted the attention of the many would-be competitors. Gannet's ability to maintain a strategy that could potentially destroy the industry structure was attributed to their having a unique set of capabilities. An effective operational network, strong local distribution and expertise in journalism, all produced a formula that could not be easily replicated by the competition. Destruction of the industry, that would follow from competitors eroding away any advantage, was avoided because the main competitors concentrated on differentiation in an attractive marketplace.

Here we have an example of a business logic that is easy to describe but difficult to implement. The business logic or approach that emerges is one that will:

- provide a profitable return while at the same time not threatening competitors in ways that will cause them to retaliate and destroy the industry structure

- enable an operation to be built that is efficient and not easily replicated or substitutable

- apply corporate expertise across the business divisions in ways that create added value for the divisions.

Starbucks and Federal Express

McGahan picks out two other companies as being successful: Federal Express, in express delivery and Starbucks in coffee retailing. We can consider these businesses in terms of how well they demonstrate that success comes from balancing strategic intent with a focus on short-term tactical actions – the Hamel and Prahalad advice. Federal Express had an average profitability around 11 per cent, average assets around $3.7 billion, revenue growth averaging at 21.6 per cent and average financial market premium at 1.07. The figures for Starbucks were: average profitability around 8.4 per cent, average assets around $0.37 billion, revenue growth averaging at 60.5 per cent and average financial market premium at 3.55. Both businesses were involved in a continuous renewal and development of core resources and capability. Federal Express built an overnight delivery service by centralizing all nightly sorting and redirecting functions at their Memphis facility. Starbucks put new stores at geographical clusters around the country. Both companies again created a tight operation around a set of unique and hard to copy set of capabilities. They adopted strategies that avoided making large pre-emptive commitments to growth but instead invested in internal developments and geographic expansion that were spread over time. McGahan suggests that the central strategic challenge for both these companies lies in finding incremental growth opportunities that do not compromise the underlying formula that has brought success.

Under-performers

Companies that demonstrate success stories give us some insight into which business logic to consider, but we can also learn from those that are seen as the chronic under-performers. In the McGahan study companies that fitted this label included both newcomers and those that are well known such as Bethlehem Steel. The newcomers included McCaw Cellular in cellular telephone service and Nova Pharmaceutical in drug research and development. Both businesses are reported as having posted below industry averages for a long period, which suggested that they had strategic problems that differed from those of their direct competitors. Both of these businesses had built major value generating assets over a long period of time. Only when the assets had been fully developed could new products be launched onto the market. For example, McCaw had to build a cellular network and create an awareness in the marketplace. Nova faced the problem of finding new pharmaceutical products. This meant years of low profits while they were building the resources, the market awareness, and the distribution capabilities that would bring returns. The risk, as McGahan points out, was that the rewards would not materialize or that they would not materialize in time. These businesses may have begun with an expectation of high performance but in the end they accepted that the investments would never be recovered. Their exit strategy was often through mergers with competitors or sell outs. The report tells us that McCaw Cellular was sold to AT&T in 1993 for $12.6 billion, in spite of their low profitability.

Older firms, such as Bethlehem Steel, can also provide some insights into how following a flawed business logic in a hostile environment can result in chronic under-performance. The history and demise of Bethlehem Steel has become the subject of many apocryphal stories in business journals. But McGahan would find many supporters to her view that the Bethlehem Steel challenges had stemmed historically from technological changes, demand swings, world politics surrounding the setting of national quotas and fluctuations in global economics. Quite a cocktail. Bethlehem, and others in the industry, had weathered these strategic challenges by rationalizing their resources and assets. In these circumstances the suppliers and customers were forced into defensive strategies to safeguard their own supply chains. Being loath to innovate or change the way that they themselves executed their business processes, Bethlehem Steel therefore had to continue to invest in the expectation that new customers would be attracted away from competitors or in the hope of forcing existing trading partners to change the way that they did business. The dominant strategy in the steel industry became one of lobbying for government support and protectionism, although this has subsequently been superseded with strategies based on the introduction of new technologies, and partnerships that have been formed higher in the value chain.

Declining high performers

As well as stars and chronic under-performers, we also have those companies that started as high performers and then went into decline. We need to see if there are any lessons to be gained by looking at their underlying strategies and the business logic that they were using. The McGahan study identified six companies as falling into the category of declining high performers. Whirlpool in major home appliances, Benihana in restaurants, Carnival Corp. in cruise lines, Coca-Cola Bottling in soft drinks, Rite Aid in retail drug stores and Snap-On in tool manufacturing and distribution. The report suggests that they all lost their distinctive performance within their industries as the features that they had used to support performance declined. In our terms we would describe this as a failure to adapt the business idea to changes in the business context. For these companies their competitors compounded the decline and eroded away any advantage that they had originally held, although the suggestion is made that the decline due to this competitor effect took place at a much slower rate. But we need to see how this came about.

Benihana operated a chain of Japanese restaurants over the period 1983 to

1992. Any reader who was in America when Benihana first opened will tell you that eating there was the "in thing." Restaurant industry profits were higher than average over the period and Benihana were among the top performers. They are attributed with being the first restaurant to introduce "eatertainment" as an additional attraction to the dining experience. McGahan refers to this as a "business specific effect" that by 1992 had ceased to give them an edge. Customers began switching to other dining and associated entertainment options that were now available. This, McGahan suggests, was not direct imitation but customers were seeking novelty and Benihana's competitors responding by providing new restaurants and other experiences. Benihana still managed to retain a core of loyal customers and suppliers which produced a medium level of profitability. But the downfall was that their success attracted attention from both existing and new competitors. The strategic challenge that Benihana faced, but perhaps did not recognize or meet, was not one of protecting themselves from imitators but competing against those who developed and innovated beyond the business idea and supporting structures that Benihana thought they had perfected. It can be argued that the decline in all of these industries was more due to the failure to adapt an original winning business idea and the change in customer perception and needs, rather than structural and environmental effects within the industry itself.

As in all competition there are, of course, those companies that can be classified as having crashed from a level of excellent performance. Many are household names and the McGahan report identifies Boeing in military transportation, Fair Grounds Co. in horse racing, L.A.Gear in shoes and others. For these companies, McGahan suggests that the industry, corporate and business specific effects all eroded quickly and dramatically. Profits declined rapidly. The timing between high and low performance was a matter of one or two years only. The rise and fall of L.A.Gear will be found as a case study on many MBA programmes. They are reported as posting revenues of $36 million in 1986 and $902 million in 1990. Their main market was teenagers and those interested in fashion wear. A simple observation would tell us that the purchasers could easily switch to another fashion supplier once they had bought into the notion of fashion in footwear. Unless L.A.Gear could move with the fashions then they would lose sales. In 1990 competition from companies such as Reebok and Nike provided the opportunity for teenagers to switch. In 1994 sales at L.A.Gear had fallen from their 1990 high by as much as 50 per cent. But L.A.Gear did not reduce investment and the levels of operation very quickly. McGahan points out that in every year between 1991 and 1994 the operating profit was negative. Competition on price and investment in specialized assets and inventory meant that the company was locked on to a formula that spelt destruction.

Declining moderate performers

Moderate performers who then go into decline can also provide some lessons as to how to interpret why a business logic that is built on low risk can also fail. The McGahan report identifies Digital Equipment in computers (now part of Compaq), Pizza Inn in restaurants, Crown Books Corp. in retail book stores, Everest and Jennings in medical equipment, Bowl America Inc. in bowling centers, and Todd Shipyards in shipbuilding, as businesses in this category. The main feature that is reported to have caused their decline from moderate to poor was industry effects. As the industry structure shifted, McGahan suggests that business specific effects became significantly and persistently negative. With these firms the strategy that was initially followed was to invest gradually so as to achieve moderate profitability. They became highly committed to positions that could not be adapted rapidly as customer tastes and supplier technologies shifted. They had become susceptible to what is known as sunk costs. There was no easy way of changing either their operations, their image or their products.

Companies which "turn around"

Companies that moved from being low performers to high performers often include those who experience and succeed at what is known as a "turn-around" strategy. McGahan has included in this category Turner Broadcasting news and the Sprint-Fon Group, the long distance communications service, Ackerley Group in broadcasting and Minnetonka in personal care products. Some of these were in so-called "unattractive" industries, with few business-specific characteristics that would indicate potential competitive opportunity. As we saw earlier, Turner Broadcasting's early lack of profitability was due to a high initial investment program aimed at future returns. With the support of a corporate parent, the company showed profits above the industry average after a few years. This in turn attracted customer interest in this new form of news broadcasting and the overall industry returns increased. The other broadcasters did not compete head on but started to produce differentiated products and services to meet the new demand.

The business logic here is one that depends on high initial investment in building brand, obtaining capital assets and then building capabilities. This results in revenue growth with a low profitability for a significant period of time. The unique capabilities are secured before the profitability levels are attractive enough to interest competitors. By that time the capabilities will have been too well embedded to make it possible for them to be imitated easily. Hence the competitors are forced into offering a differentiated service and the industry structure is not threatened. The alternative would be for the competitors to invest heavily over a long period.

McGahan quite rightly suggests that this type of business logic, where the investment may not pay off for a long period of time, relies on having a strong and supportive corporate parent. It also requires a strong business leader whose vision can survive the critique that surrounds any short-term lack of profitability.

Not all turnarounds are as spectacular as that of Turner Broadcasting. McGahan identified companies such as International Paper in packaging, Houghton Mifflin in general publishing, and Ford Motor in manufacturing autos and parts as ones where under-performance was overcome. Many of these companies had, earlier in life, exhibited advantages that had then become disadvantages. But as old and established companies they had loyal customers who were committed to the old business idea and supporting structures that the companies had been using. This, McGahan argues, made it difficult for them to change the way they worked. But over the period 1981 to 1990 these rising under-performers had produced profits that were average for their industries. They did this by seeing new opportunities and adapting old resources to a new business idea and supporting structures. Working with suppliers and customers, argues McGahan, was their path to recovery. It became imperative for them to continuously add customer value through incremental improvements, given their large asset base and investments. Radical change, for these large companies, was not an option.

What does this research tell us?

This research is significant in our search for a winning approach to business development. It shows that businesses are using an underlying logic to compete. More importantly that the logic being used varies between industries and between businesses within an industry. Some of the features of the business logic that are in use can be summarized in the following way.

Companies that eventually produced high profits but only after a long period:

- persisted in engaging in a long process of asset development and investment
- pursued creation of a difficult, and near impossible to imitate, capability and hence advantage
- increased profits incrementally and slowly over time, which did not raise undue interest from competitors
- took and managed the risks in pursuing long-term investment projects aimed at developing a new approach to providing a service or set of products
- had a supportive corporate parent.

Companies that produced low profits over a long period:

- engaged in similar programs of investment in assets and capabilities
- had ultimate business prospects which were not very attractive at the start
- were restricted in their opportunities to change operations, products and services by their previous investment in assets (they suffered from the effects of sunk costs)
- were constrained to continue with the same business idea and supporting structures by customers' and suppliers' perceptions of the business
- suffered rapid loss of revenue where there was a low cost to customers to switch to competing products and services.

Companies that showed medium profitability over a long period:

- developed their resources incrementally
- made investments that followed from growth in profitability
- avoided high growth strategies that depended on making large investments or acquisitions in uncertain conditions
- tended to be large companies from the wholesale and retail trade and from the transportation sectors.

These examples do provide an insight into how profitable and unprofitable performance of a firm can be attributed to the adherence of an underlying business logic. We can begin to see that business executives and strategists become victims of circumstances over which their influence is limited and prescribed by history. Joining and becoming the CEO of Turner News Corporation, as opposed to Beni-hana Restaurants, Bethlehem Steel or L.A.Gear would present us with an alternative set of choices, but many would be determined before we arrived. Our scope for action would be limited by the history of the company and how this had created the business logic. These prescriptions would include:

> Business executives and strategists become victims of circumstances over which their influence is limited and prescribed by history

- the way in which value was added by the business and made available to the customer
- the perceptions held by the stockholders as to the potential of the firm for producing short- and long-term profits
- the business specific effects or unique capabilities
- the structure of the industry
- the actions of the competitors themselves.

– not exactly a clean sheet from which to start our quest for fame and riches.

Given a choice we would find ourselves wishing that we were able to start from somewhere else.

The fixed plan v. flexibility paradox

The twin pillars around which business success has to be built are having a clear strategic vision supported by a strategic plan and an approach that is able to flex and respond to unpredictable events and opportunities. This presents us with a key paradox in organizational life: to proceed with a fixed plan or to rely on being infinitely adaptable. A look at some lessons from Netscape Communications Corporation's phenomenal growth, from $80 million sales to $500 million in three years, and their eventual valuation at $10 billion, on acquisition by America on Line in March 1999, shows how one company handled this paradox.

Netscape

Michael Cusamano and David Yoffie, in an article in the *California Review*, give some insight into how Netscape, the developers of the internet browser, played their strategy game. Cusamano and Yoffie identified four lessons for start-ups from their study of Netscape.

- Create a compelling, living vision of products, technologies and markets that is tightly linked to action.
- Hire and acquire managerial experience in addition to technical expertise.
- Build the internal resources for a big company, while organizing like a small one.
- Build the external relationships to compensate for limited internal resources.

This recipe is one that, they argue, enabled Netscape to grow rapidly while facing the challenges of a highly competitive market with low entry and exit barriers and major competitors such as Microsoft. Netscape also had the good fortune to hire Jim Barksdale as CEO. Barksdale had moved from sales in IBM to chief operating officer at Federal Express which he grew from sales of $1 billion to $7.7 billion and then in 1992 to McCaw Cellular Communications as president. When McCaw were bought out by AT&T he became CEO at AT&T Wireless Services. He was courted by Microsoft, who were looking for a CEO, but decided to join Netscape. Obviously he was someone who was well used to handling firms that were going through a period of rapid growth. Cusamano and Yoffie suggest that one of the strengths of Netcape's managers was their ability to make tactical adjustments.

They had become expert tacticians. They could turn short-term ideas into products and get them to market at an amazing rate. At the same time they saw long-term planning as inappropriate to the business that they were in. The rapid changes in the marketplace dictated a business logic predicated on having a six months' planning horizon. But Netscape were competing with Microsoft, who had a very systematic approach to strategic planning and to observing and managing the moves of their competitors. An interview by Cusamano and Yoffie with Microsoft's President, Steve Ballmer, indicated that while Microsoft did not support the view that the marketplace, and user requirements, were changing rapidly they were nonetheless prepared to match the game that Netscape were playing while continuing to pursue their longer-term strategic vision. Microsoft used an approach that analyzed the environment in some detail and developed plans that would both develop and shape that environment. This is an approach that we will look at in later sections, that relies on stimulating the minds of the business managers to explore the way forward while sharing a common road map and set of visions for the future. The popular press and the media tell us that Netscape, like most businesses in this industry, were meanwhile relying on one or two key players to spot the breaks and drive the company forward with the rest of the managers anticipating and encouraging this technology-driven vision. This is a culture that allows technically driven managers to concentrate on day-to-day problem solving, which is their strength. Cusumano and Yoffie comment that having left Netscape, Rich Schell, the one time head of engineering reflected:

> ❝ The Netscape product cycles were typically six months long. And we were getting customer requirements that were changing all the time. The market was moving all over the place. So we were adapting. It did not seem to make sense to have a strategy that you write down to make a decision today about something that's going to occur a year from now, especially in a market you don't understand. At the outset it wasn't appropriate. Two years into the company, it probably would have been a good thing to have a formal planning process. ❞

Here we see a perfect example of a logic being played to win and then changing as it failed to match the business growth demands. We have seen a number of businesses fail to make this change and we need to understand how this happens. The next chapter will help us to do just that. We will look at how particular strategies that are played out within this framework of logic, contribute to success. We will look to see where the logic can become so dominant that changes to strategies have little effect on business outcomes. And will consider whether business strategies have any reality or are merely rationalizations around outcomes and business performance.

Chapter **4**

The reality of business strategy

I wonder if we could contrive … some magnificent myth that would in itself carry conviction to our whole community

Plato (429–327 BC) Greek Philosopher. Republic, Bk.V

Believing in a winning idea

As we know, businesses are founded around a single business idea. The founder combines personal motivation and a vision to formulate a way of making money. As the business grows then the single idea also grows and we find that the enterprise becomes a multi-business – a business that is pursuing more than one business idea. The part played by the business idea is important because it encapsulates the unique thinking and distinctiveness of the business. It defines the source and character of the thinking from which the business logic and strategies are developed. Figure 4.1 overleaf shows how the original business idea is translated into strategies and actions that generate surplus value.

The business idea is important because it encapsulates the unique thinking and distinctiveness of the business

In Part 3 of the book we explore this notion of the business idea in more depth. But for now we want to see who drives the business development and how they go about it.

There are two groups who are playing for high stakes in the competitive business game. *Investors* who are looking for a return from having taken a risk and the *business executives* who are paid to deliver against these expectations. Both the investors and executives believe that the enterprise that they look to for wealth generation, is controllable once an underlying business logic or formula for winning has been discovered. The game can then be played by enacting strategies within that framework of logic. Subsequent fluctuations in the performance of the enterprise are then attributed to either:

- having developed and applied the wrong business logic
- having got the logic right but enacted an inappropriate strategy

Figure 4.1 The business idea and development of a business logic

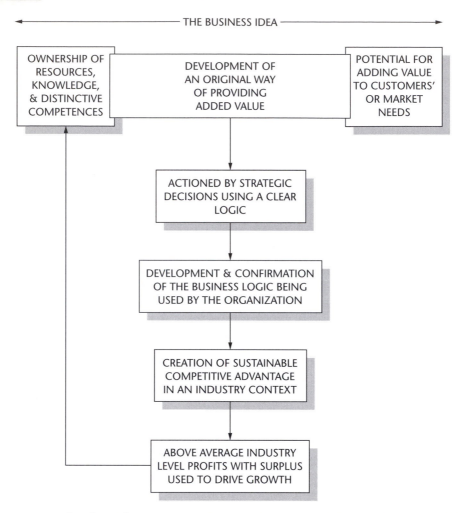

(Based on ideas attributable to Kees van der Heijden, Scenarios, *The Art of Strategic Conversation* (1996))

- the players within the enterprise having failed to recognize and play the strategy correctly (we would call this lack of control)
- the competitors having learned how to thwart our strategies
- events outside our control thwarting our play (both the logic and the strategic moves)
- the stockholders' expectations having been over ambitious in the light of a recognized level of risk
- just bad luck.

Within a business there are two contributors to this quest for lasting survival and success, the strategist and the business planner. The goal of the strategist is to be able to sense or see how to achieve satisfaction for the stockholders and a wider group of stakeholders. The planner, on the other hand, is seeking to clarify the business decision-making process and how performance will be evaluated. Acting as the lead strategist is the role assumed to belong to the directors or CEO and embraces notions of loyalty and ethical behavior on behalf of the enterprise. Whereas the planner is concerned with formulating how to describe the actions and controls that can be adopted by those running the business.

Responsibility for delivering stockholders' expectations includes ensuring that the business logic is made explicit and that strategic actions and decisions are executed as planned. The conventional view of what constitutes a good business logic and set of strategies is that they must be seen as viable by those involved in the decision-making loop. Viability here means first that the logic must fit and support the dominant views of the power group. If it differs widely then the degree of change must be justified against a perceived level of risk or benefit. Second, it must be feasible to follow the logic and implement the strategies in the light of the known capabilities and resources of the enterprise. It is this type of thinking that drives the strategist and the planner together. As the strategist moves from thinking towards making strategic decisions over investments and balancing risk with return, then the need for hard and persuasive data becomes essential. The decisions also have to be communicated to a wider group of managers and controls established over expenditure and over performance to identify variations from what was predicted. The gap between the thinking and action is thus closed. The reality of this process is that it works. But where a business begins to fail to deliver expected outcomes then the rationalization begins. The most common explanation as to why the logic failed to deliver the required performance is that the business environment changed more rapidly than anticipated. Companies rarely question the fundamental business idea that is being used. Even less do they consider whether the business logic is providing a good enough map with which to play the business game. There are a plethora of texts and techniques available that support this belief in the value of having a business logic with associated strategies. If the notion that there is a winning business logic is a myth, then we need to take a much closer look at why business managers treat it as a reality.

Why we believe in a winning business logic

Researchers and management gurus have done their best to explain how the notion of a business logic has become embedded in organizational folklore. Their argument runs like this:

Individuals make sense of organizational outcomes and take action using causal cognitive maps. These maps are used to explain and rationalize about how internal actions and external events are linked to outcomes. These maps are created and influenced by the individual's own experiences but they are also developed within a social setting. If the setting is sufficiently influential then over time the individuals will develop a shared understanding of the underlying logic to the business. An understanding that is used to respond to changes and events in the business context. As the organization exceeds or fails to meet performance expectations then the dominant business logic will be either confirmed or challenged. In order to live out the business logic, strategies have to be enacted and decisions made. Over time key enactment strategies become institutionalized and take on a significance in the thinking and processes that the managers use to run the business. Successes in performance are attributed to the effectiveness of the strategies and further confirm the astuteness of the business logic. The business logic is now rarely questioned, as it is has become embedded as "the recipe." The strategies have become management processes and are now disconnected, in the minds of the managers, from the business logic. The strategies have taken on a life of their own. It is only when disaster strikes that managers are likely to look first at the institutionalized strategies and then only if they are facing serious difficulties will the business logic or recipe be looked at and changed. Here the strategies are not being driven by perceived changes in the business environment but by managers who are focused on making the outcomes of the strategies meet internally constructed performance criteria. The organization finds it increasingly difficult to see the importance of reviewing the impact of the external environment on the business idea and the relevance of their ingrained business logic.

This line of argument and explanation would find support from the majority of academics and business managers, particularly those managers who have found themselves in positions where the external world or competitors' actions have caused their business logic to fail. There is plenty of evidence to show how this can happen.

Ford Motor Company

A classic example can be found with the Ford Motor Company back in 1920. Henry Ford took the view that there was a mass market waiting to be satisfied and that customers wanted to have a simple and functional automobile at a low price. The business idea and logic led to the following decisions:

- to design an automobile that could be mass produced
- that standardization at all stages from manufacture to sale would minimize costs

■ that the benefits from the economies of scale attached to large demand and high volume throughput would mean that Ford could beat all competitors by meeting the customer demand for low price personal transportation.

Based on this combination of business idea and business logic Ford implemented strategies that included:

■ vertical integration within the industry, both upward and downward to control the value chain and hence costs

■ standardization on a functional design that was closely linked to the manufacturing cycle

■ introduction of employment practices and management of labor that ensured control and motivation of the workforce

■ a massive investment in their River Rouge plant that created one of the world's first flow production facilities.

Ford were now the envy of the industrial world until Alfred Sloan, of General Motors, decided to compete on product differentiation. Ford were now faced with having to revise both the business idea and the dominant business logic. The strategies had been institutionalized and had now taken over from the business logic itself. They had a life and meaning of their own but the logic on which they were based was now flawed. Ford had to close the River Rouge plant for 12 months for re-tooling to be completed. Ford never regained the market leadership on the scale that they had previously enjoyed.

An example from the retail industry illustrates how following what was once thought of as a winning business logic can lead to near ruin.

The Body Shop

In 1976 Anita Roddick formulated a business logic that followed from a business idea based on a personal interest in natural products. It went something like this. The rising interest in environmentalism and the growing awareness of the abuse of animals in the testing of cosmetics and other products would push people towards natural products. The consumer markets would be attracted to products made from fruit and naturally available oils rather than those that were chemically created and animal tested. The market appeal would be worldwide and focused on women. A women's world. That her projected interest and leadership in championing this cause would provide a unique offering that was not copyable as the competitors were locked into chemically-based artificial products.

The strategies that followed involved setting up importing and manufacturing facilities and establishing a franchising business that would support rapid expansion. Over the next 17 years sales grew to $250 million worldwide and some 700 stores were operating. The growth strategy in the UK and Europe had been based on franchising, but in 1988 the company decided that entry into the USA would be through direct ownership of the stores. As the growth had been slow and the margins not particularly attractive, competition in the UK and Europe had been low. But in the USA, the largest market for cosmetics in the world, the major players such as Estee Lauder and Leslie Wexner of Limited Inc. were quick to imitate Body Shop products and establish their own stores and brands in natural products. Estee Lauder launched its Origin line of cosmetics and Limited opened Bath and Body Works to sell natural products. Body Shop quickly moved to franchising to gain a foothold in the fast growing US market but the initiative had been lost. The result was a lost opportunity to earn billions of dollars of sales in this key sector in the cosmetics industry in the USA.

Here we see that the business logic did not take into account retaliation from major global competitors. It could be argued that the strategies were sound but the business logic lacked that vital awareness about retaliation. Something that may be attributable to the beliefs held by the founder, and ingrained in the management thinking, about the infallibility of both the business idea and the logic that was being used to grow the business.

Three generic strategies

One of the strongest arguments used to embed in our minds the notion that strategies have to be found before we can compete successfully, is that there are generic strategies which are applicable to every industry and context. Further, that we have to find a match between these generic strategies and the stage of growth in the particular industry. Our strategies have to be contextualized. By doing this we will be able to achieve a winning approach, a perfect game play.

Here we see the familiar dichotomy of nature versus nurture being used to argue that a business strategy must be found that fits the particular context. No longer are we encouraged to look for a universal solution to our quest for a winning approach, but instead we are told it is all about generics and context. Intuition tells us that this is probably true. We are certainly used to adapting our approach to everyday problems according to the circumstances, so why not our business strategies? As long as we remember that the strategies are meant to be part of a long-term view and that the context will be changing over time, then the notion seems plausible. But let's have a look at some of the evidence and see how this notion progresses our search for a perfect business logic within which we can identify winning strategies.

Product differentiation

Competition has alerted the world to the profit potential attached to finding and operating in markets where customers are faced with choice. This notion leads quickly to the first of the three generic strategies, that of product differentiation. Competitive advantage is gained by designing either a product that is aesthetically appealing or one that has superior functionality. This sounds fairly straightforward but when it comes to implementing a differentiation strategy we see immediately that the devil is in the detail. For example, challenged with having to determine the functionality or design appeal trade-offs when specifying a new personal computer such as the Apple iMac, features on the SEGA Dreamcast video consul, specification of a new internet personal banking facility, a new microprocessor at Intel or the handset for the new third wave cellular phone, we would want more than a notion to sustain us. Obviously differentiation requires that we come up with a unique idea. An idea that will ensure that the product or service will appeal to potential customers but at the same time is not easily copied or substituted. If the idea is sufficiently unique a premium price can be charged. To be in a position to succeed through application of a differentiation strategy a business must choose between being able to:

The more a company can differentiate its products and services from the competition then the more successful it is likely to be

- innovate
- produce to superior quality levels
- excel in responsiveness to the customer's demands.

The more a company can differentiate its products and services from the competition then the more successful it is likely to be. Conventional wisdom would also suggest that even where the decision is taken to segment the market and focus on particular groups of customer needs, it is still important that a price premium is placed on the products. For example, Sony offers 20 or more models of television that cover the mid to high price range. But its lowest priced model is always priced higher than that of its competitors, thus emphasizing the message that Sony produces premium products. The challenge to this differentiation strategy is the extent to which its unique characteristics will prevent customers switching to a competitor's offering. The trade-off that customers make is between their loyalty to the brand and the uniqueness of the offering in meeting their needs. Competition will quickly erode away this form of advantage. Companies find that what was once seen as a unique product soon becomes a commodity.

American Express

The American Express Company was at one time a symbol of success because obtaining a green, gold and platinum card depended on income level. Famous people were used to promote the notion of belonging to an elite group, of having been accepted as a success in life. The company was able to charge the merchants and customers a high fee because of the high quality offered and the status that this conferred. Since the early 1990s AmEx has been attacked by companies such as MasterCard and Visa, who took the line that anyone can own a credit card. Large companies such as General Motors and AT&T also produced cards to promote customer loyalty to their companies. AmEx profits fell from $200 million in 1990 to a loss of $100 million in 1992.

Companies that rely on the more intangible source of differentiation such as prestige or a belief in quality and reliability seem to survive much longer. These intangibles are much easier to maintain in the minds of customers and are less easily imitated or substituted. To the customer they become tangible and real.

Cost leadership

The second generic strategy is that of cost leadership. Here we are encouraged to become the lowest cost producer in our industry. The reasoning behind this strategy is that we will be able to charge the same or a lower price than competitors while making a bigger margin. A company that selects a cost leadership strategy must avoid spending on activities and resources that promote differentiation. The game is played by watching competitors' moves and only offering functionality or features in products and services, that customers demand. Here the skill is in monitoring where customers are beginning to see previously unique offerings as commodities. The target becomes the average customer rather than those from segmented or different markets. The benefits here are in gaining the economies of scale from large throughput. The product or service is never intended to be seen as special or unique but it is able to meet the majority of the market needs at an

A company that selects a cost leadership strategy must avoid spending on activities and resources that promote differentiation

attractive price. The company develops an approach to the market that is based on being a follower rather than a leader. To succeed in this strategy a company has to innovate in areas such as internal operations, materials management and distribution. The centre of attention and focus is inwards rather than towards the marketplace.

These two strategies can, of course, be combined if a way of limiting the cost of offering a wide range of products and services can be contained. The development of flexible manufacturing technologies has made this possible. With these facilities companies have been able to offer a wide range of products and services at low cost. Whereas previously a company had to invest heavily in different manufacturing lines for small run orders, and service a wide range of customers in specialized markets, standardization was now possible. The advent of robots, just in time manufacturing and flexible manufacturing cells enabled the benefits of standardization in manufacturing to be combined with differentiation in the marketplace. Evidence of this is in the wide range of products now available at relatively low prices in cellular phones, electronic entertainment equipment and personal computers. Companies that have been successful in pursuing this combination of cost leadership and differentiation are Motorola, MacDonald's and Intel.

Market focus

The third generic strategy is that of market focus. A strategy that encourages a firm to concentrate on a particular group or segment of the marketplace. Having selected the segment and target group the decision over whether to follow a cost leadership or differentiation strategy has to be made. The cost leader in the wider market will not find it easy to gain the advantages from economies of scale and national distribution facilities, particularly where success depends on operating with low volumes and responding to sophisticated demands. Alternatively, where the approach relies on focus with differentiation, then the advantage lies with having detailed knowledge of one set of clients and being able to concentrate all the investment in differentiation. The industry market leader who is offering differentiated products and services to a large number of sectors will find this strategy hard to beat. It does, however, require a high level of customer awareness and expertise at identifying and being able to meet their requirements.

An ability to innovate enables the focused company to meet the requirements of the sector in unique ways which competitors and imitators find difficult to match. Customer loyalty is maintained and changes in supplier prices can be passed on to delighted customers. This focused approach is used by both small and large companies. For example, 3M, inventors of the familiar "Post-it Notes," have a very wide range of products that are aimed at carefully targeted sectors within an industry. The company has an incredible record for innovation. There is an extensive portfolio of products and businesses contributing around $16 billion in sales from some 40 divisions. The central competence at 3M is technical ability. Products are built on the ability to coat substrates with materials and an expertise in working with polymers. New business ventures and products are aimed at achieving 25 per cent return on sales, relying on technical advantage to create added value. A key feature of the success of the company has been the use of a new product policy that requires 30 per cent of sales to be based on new products that have been launched in the past four years. The divisions are highly decentralized and although there is a strong central technical function, they are all able to build and develop their own research and technology expertise. The ability to innovate is obviously at the heart of the success of 3M. Although selling into the office products, automobile and metalworking markets provides niche markets, the effort to stay ahead through constant innovation is enormous. This wide spread of industries and targeted segments has reduced the risk associated with a focused strategy where a niche market can suddenly disappear. The company has always focused on getting to market early, and then moving out as the product becomes a commodity and although this may not be the only way to proceed, it has proved a winning approach to date.

Applying the generic strategies

The need to constantly review and adapt the mix of these three generic strategies has become part of the business development folklore. But to do this effectively presents two key difficulties. The first is to decide which mix of these generic strategies fits the market opportunity and the company capabilities, and the second is determining when the mix has to be changed. For example, 3M might be succeeding with their focused and differentiated strategy and be able to charge premium prices, but when is it appropriate to change? If it was decided that a differentiated product had potential to appeal to a wide market, would the company be capable of achieving and sustaining a position as a cost leader? Would such a switch be possible within a prevailing organizational culture that relies on innovation? How would niche market customers react to dealing with a company that was now focused on low cost production and distribution? Companies that fail to make the correct match between generic strategies and their market context are aptly described as being stuck in the middle.

The idea that industries are at various stages in what is known as their life cycle is not difficult to accept. Coal mining, sea transportation, farming, construction and now the information industry, all demonstrate that industries follow a pattern that involves swings as well as growth and decay. This idea is quickly followed with the notion that the risks associated with following a particular mix of strategies varies over time. As risk varies, so too does the need for investment and the expected return. Once again, the nature analogy is used where industries are thought of as being at either an embryonic, growth, shakeout, maturity or declining stage. We need to see how deeply this life cycle notion impacts on our thinking when trying to determine a winning mix of the generic strategies.

Strategies adopted by embryonic and growth industries

The embryonic and growth industries such as biotechnology, edutainment and information management are characterized by the efforts of the entrepreneur, inventor and venture capitalists, efforts which are driven by a preparedness to take calculated risks with their ideas and other people's capital. The notion of companies following a first mover strategy has been captured with examples from McDonald's in fast foods, Apple with the icon driven home computer and Sony with the Walkman portable entertainment center. Early capture of fast growing markets and the ability to charge high margins quickly attracts imitators. As the industry grows, many pioneering companies lose their position, particularly where patents expire and competition innovates in the manufacturing, distribution and support service areas. Conventional wisdom tells us that to stay ahead, a first mover must consolidate early innovations into a position where low cost and differentiation strategies can be used. The options available are to:

- grant licenses to other companies and reap the longer-term reward
- invest in developing the market and establish a set of capabilities that competitors would find difficult to match
- form strategic alliances and joint ventures with other companies to develop and market the innovation.

The decision as to which route to follow depends on the extent to which the company has the capability to support exploitation of the innovation and how effective would any barriers, such as patents and know how, be as protection against imitation.

Strategies adopted by mature industries

As embryonic industries go through the growth and then shakeout stages, the notion of a mature industry emerges. Here the weaker competitors have been eliminated or bought out and the industry is now dominated by a few large companies. In addition to this notion of maturity, we are told that although there are likely to be a number of different sized groups in an industry, these can be seen as representing sets of strategic groups. Further, that the strategic groups with the largest players, and hence the largest market share, set the tone and structure of the industry through their control and influence over standards, prices and the supplier structures. This notion of maturity is very powerful, as it suggests that the dominant game being played is one of maintaining the attractiveness of the industry, in terms of it being a part of a wider profit-making network and also maintaining margins. The three areas on which companies in these mature industries focus, are to:

- keep out new entrants and thus be in a position to maintain profit margins
- avoid price wars with competitors as this would erode away the profit margins
- control suppliers and distributors.

Deterring new entrants is achieved by meeting all the demands of the industry, with constant attention being paid to product development and, where needed, innovation. Gaps in the industry, where customers' needs are not being met, will open the door to new entrants and threaten the market sector strategies that particular strategic groups dominate. Large, well-funded companies can, of course, break in, and accept low margins as the price to pay for gaining entry. Hewlett Packard's entry into the personal computer market is one such example of this strategy in action. Often a company will accept a new entrant in order to avoid a price war, relying on the stability in the industry to allow for gradual increases in prices. Non-price competition is the aim of companies in a mature industry where the emphasis is on product differentiation and gaining market share from smaller competitors. The ability of the major players to increase the level of industry output rapidly means that prices can then be lowered, making it more difficult for new entrants to survive.

Controlling both the suppliers and the distributors are key areas where strategies are used to maintain profit margins in mature industries. A vertical integration strategy will provide the ultimate control over the cost of inputs and the timing and efficiencies to be gained from distribution. Where ownership of the chain is not sought then long-term personal and contractual relationships are established. Examples of the variety of strategies in use are:

- consumer goods industries using a set of large distributors
- car companies using franchise arrangements or dealerships
- large food manufacturers delivering directly to retailers
- personal computer manufacturers selling direct to customers using mail order.

Strategies adopted by declining industries

Many companies are in so-called declining industries. Railroads, sea transport, tobacco and, in some countries, farming industries are obvious examples of how a once attractive industry can go into decline. Technological changes, social trends and changes in fashion all contribute to this decline. The two parameters companies use to determine their strategies in these industries are:

- the intensity of competition; and
- the company capabilities relative to the competition.

The intensity of competition will depend on how easy it is for a company to exit the industry, the level of sunk or fixed costs that have been committed and the degree to which the industry offerings are seen as commodities. These factors are all linked. For example, where the sunk or fixed costs are high, then high margins are required to maintain the production capacity and running costs. In the oil and many processing industries, plants need to run continuously even when demand fluctuates.

There are four strategies in these declining industries that have gained fame in many a boardroom. The first is where a company has a well-defined set of capabilities and decides to gain market share and move towards a near monopoly position. Aggressive pricing, finding new markets and acquiring established brand names in the industry results in what is known as *a leadership strategy*. The second is where a company has some unique capabilities but industry-wide competition is still very strong. *A niche strategy* is then adopted and direct competition avoided. The third strategy is known as *harvesting*, where a company has decided to exit from the industry and cuts expenditure on advertising and investment to the bone. High cash flows are obtained prior to a move to full liquidation. The final strategy is, of course, *divestment*, which relies on selling the company before the industry hits rock bottom. The success of this strategy is obviously timing and finding a buyer who accepts the seller's view of the value of the assets. So far we have seen that there is quite an impressive range of approaches that can be adopted to formulate winning strategies.

When the generic strategies don't work

The notion that there is a winning strategy for every occasion, if only it can be discovered and applied, has some pretty strong arguments in its favor. It is not difficult to find examples where companies have matched generic strategies to particular contexts and produced excellent business results. But why is it that other companies appear to fail? Should we rationalize that they were just not very good at making the link between the context and generic strategies? Simply not very good at playing the game? Or is it that our old friend, bad luck, turned up at the wrong moment? Could it be that the losers were using a business idea and supporting business logic that was either just plain wrong or that failed to stay in tune with the changing patterns in the business environment? Perhaps as a succession of strategies were applied further options became restricted and the business failed? These are just some of the possibilities for explaining success and failure of a business. But this last one, the effect where options become restricted as a result of previous game plays, is one that we need to investigate further. We need to understand how far a company is doomed by earlier game plays and whether a company follows a predictable and unchangeable trajectory.

For a business, the past becomes the present

Experience tells us that efficiency comes from knowing how to do something very well and doing it often. The one thing that businesses have to learn to do well is handle change. So unless a company continually practices and learns how to respond to changes, both internally and in the external business environment, it will eventually fail.

Companies are constantly faced with this phenomenon of change. As the environment changes, as key stockholders alter their expectations, and competitors apply different strategies, the business idea, the supporting logic, and the efficacy of key business strategies are challenged. Most companies are slow in responding to major changes in their environment, although rationalization after the event tells them that the danger signs were visible many years earlier. Conventional wisdom suggests that these businesses were locked into trajectories that exerted a restraining force on management attempts to alter course, that events in their history had influenced perceptions about the business logic and the possible remedies that could be used to improve performance. Here we see the strategic decision makers, over a number of years, creating a powerful direction to the business that often defies change. To counteract this trajectory effect we need to improve our ability to determine how current strategies are reducing the future scope for action and the opportunities for adopting new game plays. A dream that many chess players have probably cherished for years.

Mental models

Business research has shown that managerial cognition, or the mental models held, plus the industry context itself are the two major determinants in shaping the trajectory of a business. These mental maps encourage managers to sift and discriminate among the many stimuli that they receive from their environment. Weighting these stimuli and creating patterns that can be used as a basis for thinking, decision making and action. Without this facility the mass of information that managers receive would make action impossible. These mental models act as a filter to interpretation.

The danger here is that the models have been built up from past experiences and it is easy to see how they then restrict the discovery of new ways of making sense of the game. The old models continue to be used to fit the changing situation. This is not surprising and our experiences would tell us that this is quite common in business. It is also logical to see that as organizational routines and procedures become more rooted in the organizational behavior then this further reinforces the models and mind maps in use.

Recognizing this as a problem has encouraged companies to introduce processes that are used to review the need to change strategies. But the focus tends to be less on change and more on confirming that the existing strategies and routines are correct. The use of strategic planning processes that are closely linked to allocating resources and fixing budgets, is a classic example of how this culture is established. It creates what researchers have called the "competency trap," where adherence to routines reduces the likelihood that beliefs about the business will be questioned.

Containment leads to lack of experimentation and new thinking. Here we have a classic organizational paradox. On the one hand firms are encouraged to seek and follow a well-articulated business idea and develop a clear business logic and then to use this to determine the winning strategies. But at the same time they are encouraged to promote the openness, creativity, innovation and learning that will enable the firm to benefit from changes in the context and the rules for playing the game. A way of balancing the paradox needs to be found. Conventional wisdom encourages managers to set up processes that will identify anomalies in the operation of the business. The processes are used as a basis for checking out the models and ways of thinking that are being used to drive and direct the business. Linking personal rewards for the managers to these processes raises managerial expectations and avoids the complacency that comes from rewarding conformance and low risk behavior in decision making. A high turnover among key staff will also have an impact on the extent to which new learning is introduced and available in an organization. The corollary of this is that where the senior staff turnover is very high then institutionalizing knowledge becomes a problem.

Industry context

The context in which the firm has historically operated impacts on the likelihood that changes to the business logic will be made. This supports the notion that within industries and among strategic groups a recipe for how to play the game will have been established. A common body of knowledge, industry standards, patterns of competition and exchange of leaders within the industry will all have reinforced the dominant industry recipe. Businesses that deviate from these recipes will incur the displeasure of their competitors, customers and contemporaries within the firm. The stockholders and stakeholders also have a vested interest in not changing the rules of the game or the way that moves are interpreted. The trajectory is set and only near disaster performance will bring managers to take a hard look at what has become an ingrained approach to doing business. Staying on the old trajectory allows managers to focus on improving their play of a game that they understand, one that is to a large extent predictable. To change trajectory is painful and full of hidden and unknown risks.

This notion of firms creating and then following trajectories that are only deflected when under extreme attack suggests that the conventional strategic planning process is fundamentally flawed. It is a process based on being able to devise strategies that will enable goals to be achieved. But the very process creates a determinism that appears desirable but which in reality works to restrict the flexibility that is vital to success in competitive game play situations. We need to develop an approach that encourages a "search and retrieve" style of business management and to stop looking for a winning game play that can be followed with style. Style is out, flexibility seems to be definitely in. In the next chapter we will see how quickly some of these beliefs about how to develop a winning business can change, reminding us that we need to check where these beliefs have become ingrained into our approach and if they are still of use.

Chapter **5**

Why is everyone reinventing the wheel?

He that will not apply new remedies must expect new evils:
for time is the greatest innovator

Francis Bacon (1561–1626), English Philosopher

For houses the word is "location"; for business it's "context"

One of the major criticisms levelled at the management gurus and business consultants is that they are constantly reinventing their explanations as to how to play the business game. For example, what was once seen as the acme or capstone of corporate activity, strategic planning, has now been replaced with visioning, strategic intent, flexible management and probe and learn. We could be generous and argue that the latest research throws new light on old problems and as managers grow wiser then the thinking becomes more subtle and shaded at the edges. One of the most obvious, and well-loved notions, is that organizations have an ability to think and learn. But the gurus and consultants have taken things a bit further. They have built a whole belief system on the basis that organizations can be thought of as having the characteristics that we would attribute to individuals and to cognitive processes. The gurus are happy to talk about corporate renewal, learning organizations, innovative organizations and organizational processes.

A second popular belief is that there is an underlying logic to promoting a successful business, and that strategies can be followed that will realize the benefits attached to following this logic. When the logic fails our only recourse is to resort to generating complex rationalizations as to why this was so. In both of these cases we rarely challenge the basis on which the ideas have been founded.

The gurus, much like the witch doctors and medicine men of the past, will always have a place in the tribe. But if we look closer at those who argue that they have found a "winning logic" that can be used to play the business game, we soon see that these ideas often undergo radical change. For example, some

20 years ago when the boss of General Electric, Jack Welch, suggested that strategic planning was stifling company growth and scrapped what was once seen as the ultimate in professional management, the gurus, instead of fighting back, hailed him as a hero. Henry Mintzberg, and many others, have been happy to continue to move with the times as challenges to cherished beliefs are mounted. Industry itself still holds the ring when it comes to challenging conventions and the gurus and consultants are quick to align themselves with the moods and struggles of the captains of industry. But as in all things, there comes a time when failure to make it rain to order puts the rain makers in a shaky position.

The interest in a search for the ideal way to develop and manage a business began at the end of World War II. Companies benefited from an economy that was becoming worldwide and the search for ways of delivering efficient, and at the same time innovative, products was on. Strategic plans, generated and supported by management techniques that managers could follow in order to achieve success, became the order of the day. But by the early 1980s major corporations were no longer delivering the expected performance. Competition from countries and companies that seemed to be taking a less planned approach to business management raised questions over the value of these hallowed beliefs. The growth rate of alternative remedies or cures to these business failures was exponential.

Strategic planning spawned a search for logic and rationality, with a strong dose of determinism, as a way to achieve business success. Management by objectives held sway for a number of years and was supported by a move towards motivating people by providing meaningful work experiences. Learning, organizational development and the growth of a focus on uncertainty provided some good explanations as to why the earlier remedies had not worked. Business process re-engineering, quality assurance, just-in-time and managing supply chains were all valiant attempts to understand what was at the heart of business operations and activity. A widening awareness of the need to have worldwide support for environmental protection, encouraged by disasters such as that at Chernoble, soon brought the medicine men back to fundamental beliefs and the need to run businesses with an ethical stance.

Then this notion was extended to the promotion of chaos theory. Here we saw business leaders being given the ultimate explanation. A view that tells us that there are underlying structures and patterns that are stronger in indeterminant systems than in determinant ones. That by living with and accepting chaos, businesses would be better able to promote the flexibility that is so vital to beating the competition. In a rapidly changing world, recognizing that business was like white water rafting, and unlikely to bring with it the predictability of a cruise would enable business managers to behave in much more flexible ways. Ways that are much more relevant to the emerging business scenarios. Tom Peters and his utterances about our needing "crazy people for crazy times" held business leaders in a spell. They were now being told that not only was planning and determinism definitely out, but that any fool was better than no fool at all. One can imagine Brunel and Isaac Newton wondering how much longer the world would pursue this search for a winning logic to business success. But this is the game that we are now all playing and there are some rich rewards to be had.

Putting contemporary business thinking in context

It is important to remind ourselves that in this book we are discovering how to evolve an approach to managing and developing a business that bridges personal and corporate agendas. In other words, you are making your business development strategy personal. In order to create that strategy you are equipping yourself with approaches that are built on a set of generic skills. This will enable you to play the business game no matter what rules are being applied. But for our challenge to succeed, we need to understand both where these prevailing ideas about business success and a winning logic are coming from, and the extent to which they are being followed by other game players. We need to be able to place contemporary business thinking in context.

> It is important to remind ourselves that in this book we are discovering how to evolve an approach to managing and developing a business that bridges personal and corporate agendas

There is no doubt that creating and sustaining a position of competitive advantage for a business is becoming more complicated. Here I am talking about competitive advantage in the sense of being able to achieve a profit level above that of the industry average. As the context in which the business game is played changes and as the players become more knowledgeable and skilled then new game plays come into fashion. Where the level of uncertainty in the business context increases then organizational language becomes more ambiguous and takes on a much stronger significance. It is perhaps this ever heightening level of anxiety and insecurity that opened the door to those who would see themselves profiting by offering apparent solutions and remedies.

Peter Drucker with his seminal book, *The Concept of the Corporation*, written about General Motors in 1946, highlighted the power of decentralization. Here was a strategy that provided the flexibility that would enable responses and attacks on competitors to be managed effectively. Many companies have followed this advice, some have prospered, but we can see many who have found that there was probably more to the General Motors story than was ever told.

We also had Tom Peters with his advice that companies should "stick to the knitting" and not try to move into unknown areas and activities. He managed to write a best seller, but many of the companies that were held up as examples of best practice are now in dire straits. British Airways, more famous now for the painted tail on their aircraft than for their earlier slogan of "the customer is king," found that winning needed more than an image and excellent service levels.

It seems that large companies, as well as medium and small ones, are not able to find the strategies that will support their aspirations over time. What appears to be a winning logic and a set of supporting strategies that would qualify for an "A" grade on a Harvard MBA Program, eventually proves to be flawed in some fundamental way. Conventional wisdom would rationalize that it is to do with: industry dynamics, competitors' moves, substitution, imitation, culture, government policy, currency fluctuations, stockholder pressure, global trends, weak management, inappropriate structure, inability to sustain innovative processes, just bad luck; the list goes on. What everyone seems to agree on is that:

■ business is very complex
■ the problems surrounding how to select the best mix of strategies are difficult to resolve
■ the influential players often fail to see the long-term picture
■ the financial institutions are very fickle.

The increasing use of the internet and the explosion of the e-business appears to be capable of re-writing the rules of the game and threatens to destroy a vast tranche of revered business thinking. In such circumstances it is no wonder that business managers are faltering in their struggle to find the winning approach. Many would profess to accepting that at the end of the day, one is left with just trying to do one's best in the circumstances.

Is it really that dire? Do we honestly believe that waiting for "son of Peter Drucker" or "son of Tom Peters" is going to bring us the solution to our struggles? I think not. If business managers continue to believe that a quest to find the winning logic is the only path to follow, then we must accept a rapidly diminishing half-life to our beliefs about winning formula. If, on the other hand, we are willing to break this pattern of thinking then we should perhaps be looking for some fundamental, sustainable truths among the best of our great thinkers. We should be able to salvage one or two of these truths before we set out on our own journey to make strategy personal.

Has www.com made your business thinking obsolete?

Although our thinking about how to develop a business is constantly being challenged, there are some aspects that we can accept as fixed. We know that it is a game in which there are many players; that the environment in which the game is played is dynamic and there are no set rules that if followed will result in a win. The players face high levels of uncertainty and ambiguity in determining their actions and how to respond to events beyond their direct control. If we wanted a complete statement of a winning logic then it would have to specify the sequence of decisions, being made by all players, as the game unfolds. A straw poll among academics and business managers would confirm our suspicions that production of such a complete specification is impossible. Faced with a requirement to have some belief system then business managers make the most positive statements that they can about how they intend to play the game. They describe their beliefs in terms of: a vision or mission statement, the mix of businesses and their groupings, the organizational structure and a set of intentions and ambitions. Beyond this everyone knows that "no man's land" appears to be the only path ahead in their search for the holy grail. In seeking long-term sustainable profitability businesses try to be different from one another. But as it is a competitive game, in time, they end up presenting the same products or services to the marketplace. By providing the marketplace with the same products, or, worse, offering to provide more for less, they erode away the very thing that made the game worth playing: the margin. The rate at which this sameness appears depends on many factors, although the cyclic nature of economies and industries plus the aspirations and behavior of the business managers are perhaps the more obvious determinants of this process in all industries.

Perspectives

Businesses are driven by the perspectives, aspirations and experiences of their key managers. These managers have views on the rules that apply to the game that is being played, who their opponents are, and the boundaries that cannot be crossed. Two fundamental perspectives that can be seen to dominate management thinking are the *resource-based perspective* and the industry structure or *positioning perspective*.

> Businesses are driven by the perspectives, aspirations and experiences of their key managers

The resource-based perspective assumes that differences or heterogeneity between firms will lead to higher profits being made. A reliance on invention and innovation in applying the generic strategies of cost leadership, market focus and differentiation drive this perspective. The aim is to create a unique capability that can be buffered from imitation and substitution.

The second perspective is that of positioning. Here the assumption is that high profits flow from being the same but more efficient and being able to persuade customers that by using the firm's products or services they will gain added value. This perspective assumes that homogeneity and patterns of behaviors exist between the firms in the industry. That strategic groups will form naturally and those that are in the group know how to play the game. The dominant rule is to avoid upsetting the status quo experienced by members of the group and where possible the industry. New entrants seek to upset this status quo in order to take advantage of the lack of flexibility of the firms who make up these groups.

Use of language

From the above we can see that there are fundamental ways that business strategists use language to persuade and convince others that their approaches are sound. A complex and intricate language becomes the basis for dynamic behavior. Language becomes the instrument of power and control within the business. The language becomes a form of shorthand that enables actions to be taken and procedures to be followed. Organizations become streams of decision making, managers each forming their own judgements about the impact that their decisions will have on other parts of the operation and how they will be interpreted by colleagues. Language is not, of course, value free. A rich collection of mental models can be expressed through language although many are left at the tacit or hidden level. These models will cover how to:

- evaluate the performance of the firm
- describe and evaluate the performance of key competitors
- determine key goals and how feasible these are in relation to the resources and capabilities of the firm.

Many of the arguments that are hidden inside these models, are presented as dichotomies or competing alternatives. This means that further sustainable truths about business development are often obscured by the very manner in which the managers decide to present these dichotomies.

Paradoxes v. dichotomies

In trying to determine a winning strategy or make business decisions, managers find themselves faced with choices. Choices between alternative actions can either be presented as a dilemma or as an opportunity to frame the argument as a paradox. With a paradox one is not expected to make a choice over one or other of the propositions. The question is not one of having to choose one and abandoning the other. The strength of the paradox is that we accept both of the apparently contradictory propositions. This is particularly helpful in business development, where managers are predominantly using intuition and tacit knowledge that they hold about the business. If managers present their mental models as paradoxes, rather than as dichotomies, then their thinking can be transformed. For example, the autonomy control paradox presents the argument over how much freedom people should be given over the interpretation of events and decision making. As organizations grow there is a tendency to focus and control, whereas when facing a downturn the choice may be much less obvious. Making a strong argument or case for one or other of these approaches would not allow for the strengths of each to be utilized. The divisional control corporate synergy paradox is another classic. Here the competition between divisions is seen by some as a good thing that can best be managed from corporate headquarters; others would question the contribution that corporate control really makes to the success of the divisions. Once again, the leap in thinking is only possible if we develop the habit of framing dichotomies as a paradox.

One final truth about business development is concerned with how managers view the notion of companies having to constantly renew themselves. A notion that does not sit well with a belief that salvation is to be found in discovering a winning logic and then selecting the supporting strategies or game plays.

Organizational entrepreneurship

The belief is that some firms exploit opportunities for gaining profitable advantage and others do not or cannot. This has been characterized as organizational entrepreneurship, the ability to act on the opportunity that changes in the competitive environment and which original inventions create. The type of thinking that is required to overcome resistance to new ideas or changes relies on the efforts of the entrepreneur. The entrepreneur needs to either watch and wait for a discontinuity in the industry environment to occur, or to set out to create the discontinuity. Joseph Schumpeter, an economist writing in the early 1940s, called this evolutionary process "creative destruction." The two lessons that Schumpeter gave us are as follows.

■ Optimizing the allocation of resources at any one point in time is less important than allocating them to give long-term growth.

■ Business strategy and market outcomes can only be evaluated in the context of this notion of creative destruction.

Schumpeter argued for true competition to be based on competition between new products, new technologies and new types of organization that would arise. He saw attempts to define a winning business logic and then discover ways of strategizing around price, product differentiation and unique offerings as being fundamentally flawed. His concern was to argue that these attempts to find a position that could be defended and that would continue to generate profits would be bound to end in obsolescence because early mover advantage and imitation, plus changes in contextual conditions, would eventually erode away any advantage. Business managers have experienced this Schumpeterian effect in industries such as consumer electronics, fast foods and now in a more dramatic way where the internet has created major changes to the way industries operate. The e-commerce debates around: bricks, clicks and ticks, channel conflict, content provision, and transport versus access providers, are accelerating this move to change the way managers think about business development. In this new economy, competitive advantages are more quickly eroded away and the phrase "hyper-competition" is now being used to encapsulate this dynamic situation facing businesses. Many companies now embrace continual innovation and, at the right time, radical innovation, as being the main strategy to follow. Although with all recipes there is the need to exercise some caution. Radical innovations will attract new competitors to an erstwhile semi-stable marketplace and the payback from such strategic investments may take five to ten years to accrue.

> Many companies now embrace continual innovation and, at the right time, radical innovation, as being the main strategy to follow

The need for dynamic capabilities

Our final excursion into the field of sustainable truths about business development involves the notion that firms do not always select the strategies that will maximize profits. The belief here is that firms are bound or constrained by their internal processes. These are the processes that they use to make investment decisions, select methods of procurement, organize production, invest in advertising, and manage distribution. They do not naturally seek out and pursue the unusual. Observed anomalies are quickly relegated to errors or just blips that can be ignored. Businesses put themselves at risk by not investigating and pursuing these anomalies. This has given rise to the notion that businesses must create and develop what researchers have called "dynamic capabilities." But we can quickly see that dynamic capabilities will be constrained. History and previous learning will have favored incremental improvements, hence the search for new capabilities will be path-dependent. The business will also have invested in specific assets such as technology, or a series of processes that are in themselves linked to a particular product or service. The development and introduction of new products, capabilities or markets will pose a threat or even destroy an earlier capability and the associated assets. These factors will all mitigate against the business changing current capabilities and hence will eventually reduce the opportunities to compete in a context that will inevitably change.

SUMMARY

We have now completed a review of how the competitive business game is played and considered the ideas that surround finding a winning business logic. It is time to move on. You will have discovered in Part 1 how you prefer to play the business development game and compared yourself with some of the best. Lessons from leading companies have been exposed and you have had an initial introduction to the approaches that you have to acquire. In Part 2 we tested your use of logic when playing the game and looked at what the gurus can add to your understanding. Some of the contemporary business models were found to be lacking, in that they failed to produce consistent outcomes. We also explored the extent to which the quest for a winning business strategy is based on a changing set of beliefs and why this is likely to continue. Finally we extracted some sustainable truths that will take us to our next step. In Part 3 of the book, I will help you to acquire the generic skills and approaches that will enable you to develop an overarching strategy that links your personal agendas to those of the corporation. You will become your own strategist.

Part **3**

Generic skills behind
effective strategic behavior

Introduction

Nothing great was ever achieved without enthusiasm

Ralph Waldo Emerson (1803–1882)

The ingrained approaches of the professional become obvious when we observe them in action. The barrister in pleading a case, the conductor of an orchestra, rally car drivers and many others, all rely on integrating a set of discrete skills into their approach to work. Action becomes second nature and we are given a demonstration of what some have described as frozen and stored experiences thawed and applied to order.

For the professional manager there is often a much longer time lapse between the thinking, action and outcomes stages of their work. Their approaches are more difficult to observe. In this part I will show you how to acquire the six generic skills that underpin effective strategic behavior and help you to tailor these skills to your own needs and working context. The aim is to help you develop an overarching strategy that links your personal agenda with the agenda of the organization or corporate body. With these skills you will be able to:

- create better strategies more quickly
- create the right strategies for you and your business
- communicate and win support for your strategies
- develop your own strategic sense and imagination.

The first two generic skills form the basis of your strategic behavior. They are:

- developing personal strategies
- developing business strategies.

We begin by discovering how to identify and determine the goals, priorities, motives and beliefs that drive your personal aspirations. Moving on to identify and enhance your ability to understand and manage business development. It is this area that will accelerate your performance in the workplace and provide a vehicle for developing effective strategic behavior.

The next two skills are focused directly on the workplace. They are:

- influencing others
- taking action in context.

We will explore ways of harnessing your leadership abilities. We will discover how best to gain recognition among colleagues and peers. You will learn how to harness the organizational culture and handle the local power groups and the politics. Action taking is where you apply your skills and learn to balance the interests of the internal and external organizational stakeholders.

The final two skills will enable you to excel as a strategic thinker and apply effective strategies for both yourself and the business. This will present you with a challenge. You will be encouraged to take ownership of your own strategic imagination. To remove the inhibitions that constrain your true potential. These skills involve:

- learning how to adapt
- using intuition.

Adapting to changing circumstances is a key requirement of the successful business manager, as is being able to adapt as work pressures increase and career opportunities arise. This puts demands on your ability to be creative and accelerate your learning. Using intuition, which is the ultimate skill, involves vivid exercise of your powers of imagination. The key pay-off being that you will be able to create those winning breakthrough strategies.

Part **3**A

Integrating personal and business development agendas

Chapter **6**

Developing personal strategies

Emotional and fundamental beliefs

The first step to becoming good at something is to make sure that you understand and are in control of your inner self. You also need to understand the degree to which your emotional and fundamental beliefs about your work are influencing the way you think and behave. As a business manager you will often be the keeper of the corporate consciousness and it is essential that you understand how to approach that responsibility. Tackling the learning and work involved in acquiring this skill will represent a transitional period in your life. Before starting the journey it is vital that you are clear about the fundamental beliefs that will be driving your quest. The first step involves conducting a review of your past. This will enable you to see how your fundamental beliefs have taken you to where you are in life. Then you will be ready to make decisions about which beliefs have to be safeguarded and protected and those that have to be left behind. The transition from old to new approaches begins here.

> The first step to becoming good at something is to make sure that you understand and are in control of your inner self

In tackling the following reviews it is vital that you spend some time reflecting on the questions. Then make some notes, in the text. The tendency will be to press on and go straight to the commentaries that follow each section. If you allow yourself to do this you will lose much of the learning. Try to follow the process through and then decide if it has value. If you trust me and follow my advice I can guarantee that tackling the questions and then reading the commentary that follows will be of immense value. By doing this you will have established a pattern for managing the learning in this book.

Cast your mind back five years. What sort of aspirations did you have for your work and career?

_____

_____

_____

What were the main drivers behind your behavior in work settings?

_____

_____

_____

Describe the emotions that you used to feel and the fundamental beliefs that drove your behavior.

_____

_____

_____

Looking back, if there was one change that you could have made to the way that you behaved, what would that have been?

_____

_____

_____

Coming back to the current time. What aspirations do you have now for your work and career?

_____

_____

_____

Do you see the pathway to achieving these aspirations as stable and manageable, or chaotic and uncertain?

_____

_____

_____

Make a list of the key emotional and fundamental beliefs that underpin your behavior towards your work. Then decide which of these are the ones that are going to be of use in securing your future and which have to be reconsidered or set aside.

_____

_____

_____

How realistic is it to believe that you will be able to set aside these old beliefs?

_____

_____

_____

COMMENTARY

You will have found it difficult to switch your thinking from the pragmatic everyday experiences to a more reflective or imaginary state. This switching from a logical to a more visionary stance is not something that we get much chance to practice at work. The constant flow of problems and pressures that we face forces us to rely on logic and to be clear on the actions that need to be taken. We are easily seduced away from our aspirations. But here I am asking you to reflect on what has been the basis of your vision of a future for yourself, to use this review as a first step to tackling the transition where you decide to terminate one period in your life and create a new one. This means giving up many of the comfortable habits that have made it easy for you to accept that your visions and aspirations can be shelved. You have to stop accepting that work, in all its guises, is there to dominate you.

There are two factors that either affirm or destroy our visions. One is our emotional response to daily events and the other, the fundamental values that define our individuality. To be able to hold to our visions, we have to maintain and guard the sources of our sense of self-worth. Feelings of self-worth stem from key relationships that we have formed and value. It is easier to dismiss criticism from a stranger than from someone whose opinion we value highly. At one extreme, some of us are so influenced by criticism that every comment will dent our sense of self-worth; at the other extreme there are those who are able to reject all criticism. Obviously there is some middle ground to be found here.

Managing emotion

In your review you will have relied on key personal relationships that you use as reference points for your self-worth. The emotions that drive or stifle your aspirations will depend on how these relationships are used. For example, in situations where you find yourself in conflict with someone whose views you value, then to withdraw, or, even worse, to become aggressive or sarcastic, means that emotions have taken over. The more you allow this to happen the more likely it is that a reciprocal set of emotions will be raised.

Recognizing the emotion and not trying to suppress it is a key step in your personal development. You can learn to use emotions in a way that makes them your allies rather than enemies. They should be seen as alarm signals that help you to make the right moves. Where the relationship is founded on mutual respect and strong feelings of caring, it is important to air and confirm the point of conflict and then to seek ways of harnessing the tension and new ways of framing the issue. Sticking to your interpretation of the event is important, but you also need to show a genuine concern to reach an understanding. Demonstrating personal and emotional vulnerability while at the same time holding to the beliefs and strengths that you feel about your viewpoint is a paradox that we all recognize. But finding how to strike a balance in the paradox is made easier where you have both invested a lot in the relationship.

> Recognizing the emotion and not trying to suppress it is a key step in your personal development

If, on the other hand, the conflict arises with people whose views you do not value or where a relationship has not been established, then you have two choices. The first is to decide that this is the point where you begin to build a relationship; the second is to ignore the conflict and move on. If you adopt this approach to managing events that challenge your aspirations, you will have begun to take ownership of your personal development.

Beliefs and values

The second area that is at the root of your vision of the future concerns your fundamental beliefs and values.

In the review you identified the beliefs and values that underpin and drive your vision. In sharp contrast with these values is your behavior. Often we behave, or are interpreted as behaving, in ways that completely deny what we really believe in. What we want to happen and what we make happen are often at odds with each other. The reason for this is that we learn to respond to events and problems in a reactive or tactical way. We make our focus one of winning the short-term battle and seeking outcomes that are not referenced back to our true beliefs and values. The breakthrough in personal development comes when aspirations are pursued by harnessing your imagination. An imagination that is built on a solid understanding and constant reference back to your beliefs and values, no longer reacting to events and other people's moves. The central focus must be on learning how to harness the potential that is contained in these beliefs. They become the foundation stones of your strategic behavior. They are no longer a burden or weight forged from past experience that you are being forced to carry into today. Your behavior and attitudes become more in tune with your values and beliefs. People who come to know you will describe you as someone who acts with integrity. You will be able to tackle obstacles and setbacks while staying on the straight path. You may be wondering if the effort involved in creating a personal vision and maintaining it will provide a big enough pay-off.

Maintaining the vision

We are all capable of creating a personal vision and then deciding on the values and beliefs that are being used to keep us on course. Over time we learn how to deal with and use the emotions that we experience when facing a challenge or an apparent rebuff. But if we look a bit closer at this notion of having a vision, we can see that it is more about what the vision does for us rather than the beauty of the vision itself. If we set a vision and then start to recognize a gap or discontinuity between it and reality, what we must avoid is lowering the vision. Easier said than done when our concerns about the difficulties we experience tell us that the vision is unattainable. We sense that it needs adjusting and usually that means downwards. What we need to do is to transform our interpretation of what appears to be our failure. We need to harness the tension that this mismatch creates and seek renewed efforts to bring our perception of reality up to the level of our vision. We need to see the gap and the constraints that are being placed on our vision as opportunities for learning. The ability to persevere and exercise patience enables you to close the gap without lowering the vision. The challenge is to overcome the cynicism that gives you an easy way out and a chance to drop back to old ways that make life comfortable, but not rewarding. Emotional and fundamental beliefs are so important to our vision because they spell out what makes us different from everyone else. They form the building blocks for the life-story that we are writing about ourselves. All of us want something better than mediocrity, we want a life that is fulfilling and challenging to our inner selves. A vision provides the vehicle for attaining this fulfilment and helps to set personal goals against which we can measure progress.

Emotional and fundamental beliefs are so important to our vision because they spell out what makes us different from everyone else

Setting personal goals

We are all used to setting goals and objectives in business. Visualizing the end or outcome that we desire and communicating this to colleagues and subordinates is a basic management skill. Having described the outcome then action quickly follows. But where the outcomes, and the means of achieving them, are complex and bounded in uncertainty and ambiguity then we fall back on intuition. We become cautious and engage in probing and experimenting to find a way forward. But when it comes to thinking about and expressing our goals in life and our work we are much more vague. Where our lives are concerned we have almost total control over the stretch or challenges that we set for ourselves. Not something that we often experience in the business world.

In the next review I am inviting you to start with the end in mind. Having thought that through clearly you can then start to construct a plan of action that will enable you to achieve those ends. While doing this you should regularly check back to the outcomes of the previous review making sure that your personal goals and plans for action are driven by your emotional and fundamental beliefs and avoiding the trap of being deflected by old approaches that you had decided to jettison.

REVIEW 2

Write a simple mission statement for yourself. The statement can be created by answering questions about yourself such as:

- How do I want to be characterized by work colleagues, seniors and subordinates?

- What type of contributions do I want to make to the above groups?

- What major achievements am I going to be able to record in, say, three years on from now?

_____

_____

_____

Make a note of the different roles that you will have to play in order to support this statement of mission. The parts or roles that you play might include: colleague, boss, leader, change agent, counsellor, subordinate, advocate, academic, subject expert, innovator. For each key role make a note of where you feel that your ability to play the role well is limited. Then identify and note the actions that you will have to take to improve your performance and the planned timescale. Use Fig. 6.1 to capture your findings.

Figure 6.1 Roles and improvement plans

Roles	Ability to play roles	Actions required	Timescales

Based on the above analysis, use Fig. 6.2 overleaf to record the four personal goals that you are committed to achieve in the next three years. State for each goal:

- why it is important to you
- the tangible pay-off to yourself
- the tangible pay-off to others
- where you can see yourself being put at risk
- the impact that your pursuit of these goals will have on others
- how you will anticipate and manage that impact
- where you will need support and how you will justify asking for that support
- the key steps and actions required to secure each goal
- how you will evaluate progress
- the timescale for each goal to be reached.

Figure 6.2 Personal goals

	Goal 1	Goal 2	Goal 3	Goal 4
Importance				
Pay-off to you				
Pay-off to others				
Risk management				
Impact on others				
Managing the impact				
Support required				
Actions required				
Evaluating progress				
Timescales				

Commentary

Your mission statement represents a declaration of what you want to be and the achievements that you are prepared to strive for. Clarifying the fundamental values used to create this statement will have helped you to overcome the cynicism that bedevils reviews such as this. By committing yourself to writing a mission statement your vision for the future can now begin to take shape. It may take four or five rewrites before you are confident to begin thinking about the roles and actions that follow. This is quite normal, as it is the reflection process that helps to prioritize and structure your vision. The process is one where you are allowing the tensions between your inner-self and the world that you experience daily to surface. By allowing these tensions to surface, and confronting them, you will gain the strength and insight that is essential for effective personal development. You begin to link fundamental values and beliefs to behavior. Your sense of mission will become apparent to those who you work with and form your close social group.

Balancing the roles
The notion of having to play many roles in life is well established. But it is difficult to achieve a balance between these roles in our work and personal lives.

The popular press and management magazines are quick to tell us how top people manage their working week. The conventional view is of an executive who awakes before dawn and after exercising travels to the office and works till late, fitting in a host of engagements and playing many roles during the day. Only at the weekends does this busy executive manage to find time to be with family and friends. But the trend is now to describe the executive, a Bill Gates, Richard Branson or Percy Barnevik, as someone who is able to integrate work and life. You need to be quite honest with yourself here. If it were easy to balance home and work then everyone would have learned how to do it by now. It is extremely difficult and the best advice is to go back to your fundamental emotions and values. If you decide that you really value your work life more than your home or social life then you need to be open about it and seek either support or acceptance. Setting out to pretend, or worse, to manipulate others into believing something that you know is not fundamental to your inner beliefs is a recipe for disaster. On the other hand, if you truly believe that a balance can be struck then you need to be clear about the various roles that you have to play in life. This will help you avoid becoming too focused on one at the expense of the others.

Roles, goals and the mission statement

By putting your roles and personal goals together you will see how the mission statement can be realized. You recognize the structure within your mission and actions will follow naturally. The personal goals allow you to focus on outcomes rather than actions.

One of the difficulties in setting goals is to know how specific they should be and their time horizon. I asked you to adopt a three-year timescale as this forces you to confront the uncertainties and ambiguities that the future presents. In order to set these goals you have to decide what is important to you and relevant to achieving your mission. Goals are of little use if they are vague and so general that they can easily be judged to have been achieved, for example, to succeed in my job, to develop an effective team, to grow the business and maintain profitable margins. At the same time they should not be easily attainable and superficial, for example, to enjoy my role as a manager, to reduce the stress that overwork is creating. Your goals must express a level of commitment and be stretching, but grounded in a reality that makes them feasible. Goal setting helps you to bring out what is important in your life. But you also need to be aware of the risks involved and how to manage them, as this creates a sense of purposefulness that people will recognize and respect.

The impact on others

It is also likely that within the organization there will be some who will find that your new direction and convictions conflict with their goals. Their expectations as to what you should be doing in your work and career, may be at odds with yours. You therefore need to think through carefully the impact that your new found direction will have on others. It is likely that you will need help and support in achieving your goals and pursuing your mission. It is important therefore that you discuss them with close friends and colleagues. Make sure that you are sufficiently committed and determined to pursue your goals before exposing them to others. This will put you in a much stronger position and ensure that the outcomes are focused on your vision and aspirations for the future.

Take a flexible approach

One final point is to caution you about the trap of setting goals that are too rigid. Personal development is a learning exercise and as your actions unfold it is important that you demonstrate flexibility. Focusing too much on rigid goals will cause you to lose the very spontaneity needed to see the opportunities for learning. As you progress towards your goals it becomes increasingly important to use intuition and imagination to visualize and capture the changing patterns that arise. You need to develop the skill of being able to balance goal setting and clarity of purpose with a preparedness to respond to unfolding opportunities. How you approach this balancing act will depend a great deal on your personality and cognitive style.

Personality and cognitive style

Most managers have completed an evaluation of their personal profile either as part of a job selection process or in the context of a management program. There are many variants of these tests and no doubt you have opinions about their value and validity. Psychologists and researchers use the outcomes of these tests as indicators of how we approach and tackle problems. What is important here is to recognize that these notions of differences in personality and cognitive style are widely accepted as fundamental to understanding how we behave. We need to see what they have to offer. Obviously it is not possible to provide a complete profiling test in a book such as this. I have therefore presented an overview of the personal characteristics that can be determined from using two of the more valuable tests. A full reference is provided as to the sources of these tests and I would encourage you to use these contacts to obtain a thorough professional assessment. The two reviews below are based on the following tests.

- **The Myers-Briggs Type Indicator** (The Myers Briggs Type Indicator and MBTI are registered trade marks of Consultancy Psychologists Press, Inc.) Tests can be obtained from Oxford Psychologists Press, Lambourne House, 311–321 Banbury Road, Oxford, OX2 7JH, UK, and from Consulting Psychologists Press Inc., 3803 East Bayshore Road, Palo Alto, CA 94303, USA.

- **The Kirton-Adaptation-Innovation Inventory** developed by Michael Kirton. Tests can be obtained from Occupational Research Centre, Highlands, Gravel Path, Berkhampstead, Herts, HP4 2PQ, UK, and from Management Development Institute, Eckerd College, 4200 54th Avenue South, St Petersburg, Florida 33711, USA.

REVIEW 3

There are four pairs of preferences shown in Fig. 6.3. Consider which description comes closest to your self-perception, e.g. E or I, S or N, T or F, J or P. Then decide which of the combinations shown in Fig. 6.4 gives the best fit and discuss your findings with friends and colleagues. Also make a note of areas where your personality type preference may lead to a bias in the way that you tackle work problems. Remember that I am only providing you with an overview and that for a professional evaluation you should contact the above institutions.

Figure 6.3 Personality traits

Extrovert (E)	Introvert (I)
– Favoring action	– Like quiet
– Impatient	– Forgetful of people
– Interested in others	– Work alone and like it
– Impulsive	– Hate interruptions
– Like being in a group	– Learn by reading
– Prefer talking	– Dig deep
– Like collaboration	
Sensing (S)	**Intuitive (N)**
– Like routines	– Always trying to improve things
– Applying learning quickly	– Works in fits and starts
– Good at estimating job times	– Like working to hunches
– Logical	– Tend to over complicate
– Good at precise tasks	– Questions the status quo
– Accept the current realilty	
– Like getting the facts	
Thinking (T)	**Feeling (F)**
– Like to establish order	– Avoid conflict
– Like to be treated fairly	– Like praise
– Clumsy with people's feelings	– Like pleasing others
– Good at analysis	– Sensitive to own impact on others
Judging (J)	**Perceiving (P)**
– Like to plan	– Wait for the last minute
– Like to compete	– Adapt to the situation
– Finish one job at a time	– Indecisive
– Prepared to start work without all the facts	– Avoids unpleasant jobs
– Methodical	– Work well under pressure
	– Use checklists
	– Inquisitive

Figure 6.4 **Personality – the combination of traits**

Extrovert (E)	Introvert (I)
Motivated by the external world. Make sense of the world by talking to others.	Focus on their inner world. Use their own mind as a source of inspiration. Like working quietly with no interruptions before checking out ideas with others.
Sensing – thinking types (ST) Systematic and like using proven data. Seek order and control. Averse to risk and seek cause and effect patterns. Focus on today's problems.	
Intuition – thinking types (NT) Seek unique patterns in data. Take risks in their thinking. Enjoy reducing problems to simple points. Teneency to appear impersonal.	
Sensing – feeling types (SF) Emphasize people's opinions in decision making. Focus on the short term. Like to be in harmony.	
Intuition – feeling types (NF) Project personal views as facts. Avoid using rules for decision making. Include people when structuring problems. Like breakthrough and new ideas.	
Judging (J) Prefer to work in planned ways. Emphasis is on controlling work through organization and structure. Want to decide finish and move on.	**Perceiving (P)** Prefer to be flexible and spontaneous. Want to understand rather than control. Confident that they can adjust to the context in which they find themselves.

COMMENTARY

It is likely that the review of your personality profile provided few surprises. Being aware is one thing, but perhaps the real challenge is to decide where changes can be made to improve your ability to tackle problems and work with others. Assuming that you subscribe to the notion of people having personality traits, then it is important to recognize how these traits influence approaches to problem solving and planning. A widely-held view is that people with different personality types develop dominant decision-making styles and distinctive approaches when tackling activities such as collecting data, and generating and evaluating options. These personality types will thus have inherent biases when analyzing and appraising strategic issues. For example, **Sensing** (S) dominant types seek precise data, convinced that they are realists and concerned with immediacy, whereas **Intuitive** (N) dominant types want to understand the wider picture and are happy to use more general data. Also **Thinking** (T) dominant types use logic combined with formal reasoning and prefer to generalize. The **Feeling** (F) dominant types use value-laden approaches and emphasize the more personal aspects when making decisions. These traits can be combined into four personality types:

- STs rely on systematic decision making using hard data. Their focus is on the problems of today.

- NTs stress analysis but they take leaps into the unknown. Their interest is in simplifying complex problems. They are often considered to be impersonal.

- SFs emphasize people's opinions and seek harmony. Their focus is on the short-term problems.

- NFs stress judgement and value experience. Their emphasis is on broad themes.

As an experienced manager your personality bias will by now be ingrained. You have your own way of approaching problems and we need to look at the impact of your bias. Figure 6.5 overleaf gives some examples of how this bias could be working for and against you. From these you will be able to identify where you need to focus your development. Make a note of the potential weakness in your approach and reflect on how patterns in your behavior have developed over the years. A step in your personal development will be to compensate for this ingrained bias.

Figure 6.5　Personality types and problem-solving bias

Personality type	Potential weakness in approach	Bias at the data gathering stage	Bias at the decision-making stage	Bias when testing the outcomes against intentions
ST	Uses proven approaches and rejects novel ones.	• highly analytical • ignores ambiguous data	• conservative and short term • risk averse	• locked into initial preference • over simplification • rejects evidence that does not fit
NT	Adheres to previous beliefs.	• seeks patterns • over complicates • ignores contradictory data	• long term view • preference for innovation	seeks to confirm own preferences.
SF	• favors consultation • focus on discussion at the expense of ideas	Seeks emotional data.	• emphasis on people • preference for short-term solutions that are acceptable to others	Seeks social approval.
NF	• uses imagery and vivid data • rejects standard problem solving approaches	• uses personal judgements and values • reduces uncertainty • relies on analogies	• innovative • offers many solutions to obtain best fit	Tests beliefs and view using imagery.

This next review will give you an insight into your creativity and cognitive style. This understanding is vital as your creative ability impacts on your strategic behavior and your approach to business development.

The theory developed by Michael Kirton suggests that everyone can be seen to operate on a measured scale from what he has described as highly adaptive in style preference, to highly innovative, when tackling complex issues. Adaptors are those who prefer to improve on existing practice and innovators are those who prefer to reframe problems in ways that often confront conventional wisdom. Figure 6.6 will give you an indication as to which of these styles you exhibit.

Figure 6.6 **Adaptor and innovator responses**

The high adaptor response to problems	The high innovator response to problems
Characterized by precision, reliability, conformity, methodicalness and prudence.	Seen as undisciplined, thinking tangentially, approaching tasks from unsuspected angles.
Seeks solutions to problems in tried and understood ways.	Often queries the problem's basic assumptions. Manipulates problems.
Reduces problems by improvement and greater efficiency, maintaining continuity, stability and group cohesion.	Is a catalyst to settled groups, irreverent of their consensual views. Is seen as abrasive and creates dissonance.
Challenges rules rarely, cautiously, usually when supported.	Challenges rules and consensual views.
Produces a few manageable, safe and sound ideas.	Produces many ideas, but these are often seen as irrelevant, unsound and risky.

It is important to note that someone who has a high match with one style can exhibit the other style if this is a requirement of their job. But that the stress required to maintain this adopted style increases with time and eventually impacts on both physical and mental health. A simple check can be made on your preferred style, as opposed to the style that you may be adopting, by completing the following exercise.

REVIEW 4

Reflect on a situation in your work where creativity – the ability to come up with a new way of tackling a problem or situation – was required. In this situation:

- How important was it to generate a completely new or fresh approach?
- Did you approach this in an adaptive or innovative way?
- Was this your preferred style?
- Was it the most appropriate approach in the circumstances?

■ How could you have led or initiated an alternative approach?

_____

_____

_____

When tackling business issues we are often confronted with a set of open ended and complex problems. Our cognitive bias determines where we start our search to make sense of such problems. Some managers adopt an approach that favors adaptation of the current situation, an incrementalist approach. Others question and challenge the boundaries and constraints surrounding the problem. Both approaches can be used in a complementary way but the clash of styles, for example, when working in teams, will be evident. An innovator among a group of adaptors would experience a level of rejection and become frustrated with what appears to be a painstaking approach. For the adaptors the innovator appears unrealistic, emotional and unable to communicate clearly. Recognition of the differences does not result in harmony but does open up the opportunity to combine the strengths of both styles. Innovators are often seen as abrasive in that they appear to be attacking the consensus views favored by the adaptors as well as other innovators. The initiating innovators may appear oblivious to the disruptions caused. The adaptors, on the other hand, find it easy to combine with others in the team as they are prepared to work from the point which others have established. The predominant culture in an organization and the nature of the task can require that the innovator has to behave in an adaptive way or vice versa. It is no surprise that managers gravitate to organizational environments that suit their style. The more innovative towards turbulent or less stable situations and the more adaptive to those that are predictable and certain. As you can see, it is important that you recognize your own style bias and that of your colleagues. Style becomes a strength to be harnessed rather than simply representing a clash of personality.

SUMMARY

These reviews have given you an opportunity to take a close look at the personal characteristics that underpin your approach to work situations. Your emotional and fundamental beliefs can now be used to drive and sustain your vision for the future. The feelings of self-worth that you have can now be sustained in the face of setbacks and criticisms. You can begin to accept the vulnerability that follows from letting your emotional reactions surface, while still holding true to fundamental beliefs. Clarifying goals for the next three years will have set you some stretching targets and the means to evaluate your progress. This clarification of mission and purpose will quickly communicate itself to colleagues and establish your integrity in their eyes. This will give you the strength needed to combat the cynicism that bedevils so much of organizational life. You will have determined the priorities in your work and taken the major step in declaring these decisions and handling the consequences and trade-offs that have to be made. Finally, the review of your personality and cognitive style will have given you a good understanding of your natural bias. It is important to start out with a determination to harness your natural strengths while being mindful of how they at times deflect you from the true path. We can now move on to look at the second skill, that of developing business strategies.

7

Developing business strategies

Matching strategic thinking to the business context

In this section we explore how you approach making sense of the complexities and ambiguities that a business situation presents. I have called this your business logic. The personal logic that you use to structure thinking about a business, its context, sources of competitive advantage and hence profit, in such a way that it makes sense. The quest to define the business context has spawned a plethora of techniques and approaches. The dominant belief is that we should search for the key features in the business environment, establishing their patterns as a sequence of cause and effect, or linked relationships. That armed with this insight we can then use experience and a knowledge of how the organizational capability and market need are being linked to determine actions and secure profitable outcomes. This becomes the business idea. Figure 7.1 overleaf illustrates this notion of a business idea being set in a specific business context.

Understanding how the business idea can be applied and managed in context provides the clarity needed when playing the competitive business game.

Understanding how the business idea can be applied and managed in context provides the clarity needed when playing the competitive business game

Strategies are then triggered by this understanding of a business idea that is being applied in a clearly defined context. A business logic begins to take shape through the decision making and actions that

are then played out. This is the approach that characterizes the business development process and the cascading of models used in this process is shown in Fig. 7.2 overleaf.

When our business logic results in failure to make sense of the situation and actions do not lead to success, we attribute this to bad luck. Sometimes

Figure 7.1 The business idea in context

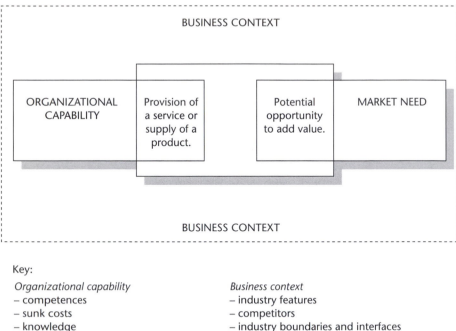

BUSINESS CONTEXT

| ORGANIZATIONAL CAPABILITY | Provision of a service or supply of a product. | | Potential opportunity to add value. | MARKET NEED |

BUSINESS CONTEXT

Key:

Organizational capability
– competences
– sunk costs
– knowledge
– experience
– networks and alliances

Business context
– industry features
– competitors
– industry boundaries and interfaces
– government and legislative features
– market structures
– technology features
– sources and structures for funding

we even blame colleagues for their lack of support. Occasionally we will admit that our personal logic needs revising but more often remain convinced that our interpretation of the situation was fine. The game was lost because we were playing against stronger, better equipped players.

My first point is that the value of an analysis of the business context is only realized when you take action based on that analysis. The analysis itself does not make the context real in any objective sense. The second point is that there are no rules for making an above average profit in an industry but that there are general rules for improving your chances of making a profit. The third point is that an analysis of the business context must be based on a clear understanding of the business idea that is driving your quest to make above average profits. These three propositions need to be checked out in your work setting so that they start to make sense. I have provided you with a series of questions and steps that are focused on creating a match between your approach to developing your business and the business context. I have delib-

Figure 7.2 The cascading of models in strategy making

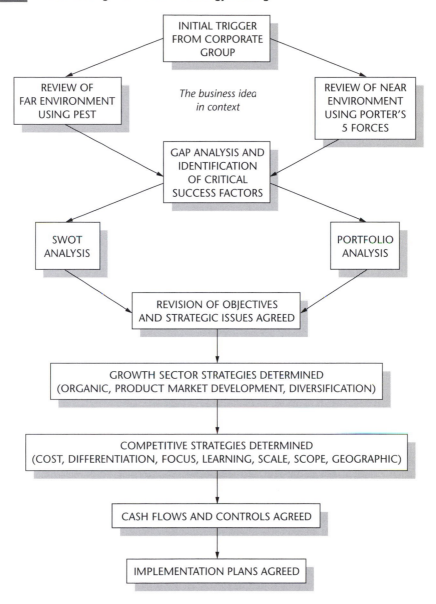

erately avoided providing you with a case study and am asking you to focus on your own company or business. In this way you will have access to the data that is required and an insight that is totally within your control. The pay-off of this next review is that you are developing a unique and personal strategic behavior.

Select a business that you are going to use for this review. Where your company is a multi-business then decide which business will best lend itself to the review.

Describe the underlying business idea that is being used to drive the business, i.e. what are the potential customer needs that defines the opportunity to add value, and what capability or combination of capabilities are being used to provide that added value? Note that a capability is made up of competences, sunk costs, assets, knowledge, experience, networks and alliances, etc.

_____

_____

_____

What mix of the following generic strategies is being used to pursue competitive advantage?

- Being the lowest cost producer.
- Identification and defense of a market niche.
- Total market coverage.
- Product and service differentiation based on incremental innovation.
- Product and service differentiation through radical and breakthrough innovation.
- Continuous learning and innovation at all levels in the organization.

You may find it helps if you rank the above as being high, medium or low in terms of their priority and evidence in the organization.

_____

_____

_____

Draw a diagram to show how the main processes in the organization, are configured and linked in order to deliver the added value to customers. This will include the processes aimed at:

- research and development
- procurement
- converting materials and items to provide products and services
- distribution

- delivery

- after sales service.

You may also find it helps to show on the diagram, how support services, such as information management, recruitment, promotions and marketing help add value.

The processes involved in creating and delivering added value

Describe the main boundaries of the industry or sector in which the business is competing. This will include geographical boundaries, technological fields, capital investment sources, customer and market segments, etc.

_____

_____

_____

Identify what you consider to be the five major industries or sectors that interface to but are outside the boundaries that you have described above. These will include industries that supply and those that use your products and services. They would also include those that are serving your customers and markets but use different technologies, media and skills.

_____

_____

_____

List the features that characterize the state of development and dynamics that exist within the industry or sector. This will include features such as: the stage in the industry growth cycle, the rate of introduction of new technology, trends in customers' expectations and needs, cost competition, international competition, government action, demographics, etc.

_____

_____

_____

Describe in a single sentence, the formula or recipe that captures the current wisdom as to what makes for success in the industry or sector.

_____

_____

_____

List the critical ingredients or factors that are needed if a company wants to succeed in the industry or sector, i.e. what does it have to have in the way of resources, competences, capabilities, image and networks?

_____

_____

_____

How does the business performance compare with that of key competitors in terms of financial and market share criteria? You will find it helps if you restrict this to comparing trends in: market share, new product or service development time, profit margin (profit before tax divided by turnover), utilization of assets (turnover divided by fixed assets plus current assets minus current liabilities), debt to equity ratio. Also fluctuation in share price and price to earnings ratio over the last 12 months. Use Fig. 7.3 to summarize this analysis.

Figure 7.3 Comparative business performance

	Own organization	Competitor 1	Competitor 2	Competitor 3	Competitor 4	Competitor 5
Market share						
Development time						
Profit margin						
Asset utilization						
Debt to equity ratio						
% variation in price earnings ratio over last 12 months						
% variation in share price over last 12 months						

You have now made sense of how the business idea is being applied in the business context. The next step is to use this understanding to develop your approach to developing the business. By addressing the following questions you will begin to see where there is a need to refocus attention in order to pursue business success.

Make a list of the key areas in the business context that you feel most uncertain about in terms of their nature, form and likely impact on the success of the current business idea.

_____

_____

_____

Using this list, decide which of these areas are essential to the development of the business over the next three years.

_____

_____

_____

COMMENTARY

In conducting this review you were faced with having to make choices about the sophistication and level of your answers. The sophistication can derive from the detail but it can also come from making a unique interpretation based on observations. When analyzing a business context you put yourself in the position of the artist who has to decide what representation to make of a set of personal observations. Deciding on the setting in which the subject is to be framed and observed. What is left out rather than what is included is a reflection of the message that you, as the artist, are trying to convey. The point that I am making is that there is no such thing as a truly objective interpretation of a business context. In this case the business context is the setting and the subject is the business idea. But it is the original business idea that must drive the purpose of your observation. What was Michaelangelo trying to say, what was Constable trying to convey, what did they think would work? They used their personal logic to make sense of the context and then used it to convey a message. Making observations without clarity over your business idea is of little value. What you include and how you represent the business context must be based on reflecting your business idea. Some contextual features will be more significant than others. If the significant features of the context are missed out then the picture that you are trying to bring to life will be a failure.

There is no such thing as a truly objective interpretation of a business context

You may also have discovered that the current business idea is out of tune with the context. This is quite different to the situation where a core business reaches maturity. The notion of maturing suggests that the business has used up all opportunities for growth in a particular context. But where a business idea is out of tune with the context then the opportunity to reach maturity no longer exists. The growing, flowering and dying plant metaphor only distracts the analyst from what is often the real cause of a business failure. Failure occurs when the business idea is no longer deliverable within the particular business context. Continuing to interchange and prioritize generic strategies will only delay the point where the business idea has to be modified or abandoned. One of the classic mistakes that most businesses make is to either misread the changes in the context or to make decisions that pitchfork the business idea into a different context. A context in which the business idea can no longer flourish. The outcome is that the business fails, as the original idea can no longer deliver the required value to customers. This phenomenon has not been given much press because the corporate strategist, like the cottage gardener, solves the problem of misfit by managing a number of partial misfits, in order to spread the risk. Or, alternatively, has plants in the pipeline that are used to provide a sequential display of success. This interplay between the business idea and observations about the business context create the basis for decision making about how to develop the business. Gaps in performance and responses to perceived changes provide the stimulus to action. Your identification of the key areas that are likely to impact on the business idea and decisions to change the idea, form the base for the next review: that of how to link business development to implementation.

Linking development to implementation

In this section we use the analysis of the context and elements in the business idea to determine the options for developing the business and how to implement them, remembering that it was your business logic, how you make sense and find patterns in business situations, that enabled you to describe the context. Your ability to generate options and to be clear about implementation will also depend on your position within the business. As an owner you will be under pressure to

It is the subtle interplay between the business idea, the business context and the business strategies that creates the foundation of a successful business

select options that balance with your financial commitments and personal preparedness to take risks. Whereas as a business manager, the drive may be much more to do with your closeness to the stakeholders and to the corporate group. But in either case, the approach that you adopt may involve making changes to the business idea, the way that you are adding and delivering customer value, or changes to the dominant business strategies. It is the subtle interplay between the business idea, the business context and the business strategies that creates the foundation of a successful business.

REVIEW 6

Use Fig. 7.4 overleaf to capture your evaluations of which groups are the main beneficiaries from the activities of the business. Start by describing the four key

117

Figure 7.4 The stakeholder analysis

	Stakeholder Group 1	Stakeholder Group 2	Stakeholder Group 3	Stakeholder Group 4
How does the group provide financial and tangible inputs to the business?				
How does the group make intangible contributions to the business?				
How is the group able to operate independently of other stakeholders?				
What are the dominant criteria the group uses to judge the business outcomes and performance?				
What is the relative importance of the group in terms of its ability to influence business outcomes?				
What are the key values and beliefs of the group?				

stakeholder groups. The focus here should be on the groups that view the business as an entity that provides a financial or political return for their investment. The shareholders would be an obvious group to include.

Use the stakeholder interest and satisfaction analysis, plus the review of the business performance, to identify which areas of performance need attention. It is important that you provide details of the associated performance parameters, as these will be used to evaluate both gaps and expectations in performance. List these areas and the associated parameters in terms of those that are:

- critical and in need of rapid improvement if the business is to survive beyond 12 months
- essential and in need of serious attention if the current business growth rate or market position is to be maintained over the next two years
- essential and will require some breakthrough thinking if the business is to become or continue to be a dominant player in the industry or sector over the next three years.

Use Fig. 7.5 to record your thinking about these potential areas for development.

Figure 7.5 Business development – identification of key areas and performance parameters

	Business Areas	Performance Parameters
Critical over next 12 months.		
Essential for continued growth over the next two years.		
Essential for breakthrough and dominance over a three year time frame.		

Refer to the description made of the business idea in Review 5 on page 112, and then answer the following questions.

■ Where there are gaps between desired and actual performance, which of the following do you consider has created these gaps:

(a) the business idea failing to provide the required added value to customers?

(b) failure to determine and apply the correct mix of strategies?

(c) failure to have anticipated the impact of events such as: fluctuations in the economy, competitors' moves, developments in technology, changes in customer loyalty?

(d) failure to provide the structural and financial support required by your business idea?

(e) failure to implement the intended strategies?

_____

_____

_____

Based on the above analysis and that completed in Review 5, make a list of the key issues facing the business. These issues will have arisen from:

■ an analysis of the expectations and interactions of the key stakeholders

■ views on how well the business idea is succeeding in terms of making money and sustaining business growth

■ a review of business performance in key areas

■ a consideration of the industry dynamics and the impact of potential changes in the wider environment

■ a view as to the effectiveness of the current mix of strategies that are being pursued by the business

■ an analysis of key competitors in terms of: their dominant business idea, performance and key strategies.

Use Fig. 7.6 to help capture these findings in terms of their importance to the business over the next:

■ 12 months

■ three-year period.

Figure 7.6 Key issues facing the business

Issue	0–12 months	12–36 months

You can now decide which areas of the business idea have to be modified and where changes to the current strategies are required.

Modifications to business idea

_____

_____

_____

Changes to the mix of strategies

_____

_____

_____

Reflect on the feasibility of implementation of the changes that you are proposing. Ask yourself:

■ are they clear, robust and aimed at meeting the expectations of the key stake-holders?

■ has the associated risk been anticipated and can it be managed?

■ will they promote competitive advantage?

- what skills are required for implementation and are these available within the business?

- what support and help will be required to ensure effective implementation?

Make a note of the key points from these reflections.

_____

_____

_____

COMMENTARY

It is impossible to prove that the performance of a business is directly linked to any particular strategy or set of strategies that are being pursued. The interactions between the strategies and their relative impact on business outcomes are, at best, not understood. Furthermore, strategies are usually derived from a mixture of intuition and experience. The decision as to which option to pursue is usually made using explicit criteria to evaluate the alternatives. The criteria selected are those that take into account the impact of each option on the various stakeholder groups, the competitors, the marketplace and the industry. In an ideal world this could be turned into a fair and open process of decision making. The reality is that the decision makers hold strong beliefs about the priorities of one or more of the stakeholders and the relative importance of the criteria being used. Hence strategic behavior becomes characterized as one where managers are using their best judgement. We learn to balance short-term business pressures with the longer-term interests of the business. These decisions create the business outputs and set up demands for resources and how they are obtained and deployed. An additional balancing act is also required between the interests of the owners or shareholders, the investors and bankers, the managers and staff, the public at large, the industry regulators, and government institutions. It will come as no surprise that best judgement again plays a big part in how this balancing act is conducted.

The review of the business performance will have highlighted where the business idea is no longer in tune with the business context. Failure of the idea can arise as a result of a whole raft of events from fundamental changes to customers' expectations about added value, to industry deregulation and changes to technology in the industry. A good example of this is the retailing industry, which is being challenged by the growing influence of the e-commerce activities. Being able to link your thinking about the business idea to concerns about which competitive strategies to pursue, is a key skill that has to be developed. Armed with a keen understanding of the operational and strategic issues, the decisions as to what mix of strategies to pursue becomes straightforward. Changes to structure and organization can then be determined, along with checks on the barriers that will have to be overcome during the implementation process. Completing this review will have challenged some tried and tested methods that you have relied on in the past. But it is also important to value past experiences, and in the next review you will have a chance to do just that.

Valuing and learning from experience

As a manager you will have been exposed to a wide range of experiences of how the business development process operates. You will no doubt have seen some well-designed and articulated processes that produced poor outcomes, plus some almost non-existent processes that arguably resulted in success. One of the major difficulties we face is how to learn from these experiences. The time-lag between making a business decision and evaluating the consequences is often quite long. Negative outcomes, as we have seen, are easily rationalized as being due to unpredictable events that occurred outside the organization. We also know that as successive decisions are made, the opportunities for major changes are inevitably reduced. The notion of sunk costs, creation of an organizational image and reputation plus the development of a dominant and distinctive culture remind us that we rarely start with a blank sheet. The question here is: are we doomed by our past or can we learn from our experiences? Learning how to benefit from the investment that previous managers have made in the organization, and from personal exposure to the industry, is a skill that you need to acquire. The following review will help accelerate that learning process.

REVIEW 7

Looking back over the past five years, list the experiences or events that have had the greatest impact on how you approach making sense of and finding patterns in complex business situations, i.e. your business logic.

_____

_____

_____

Has the business direction – how the business is being developed and grown – been established from the top down, or has it arisen as a result of the thinking and action from the middle or operational management?

_____

_____

_____

Rank the following in terms of their influence on the approaches taken to grow the business.

■ outside events, for example, competitors' actions and changes in how the industry operates

■ inside politicking

■ the ability of the organization to perform at the functional levels

■ the internal management processes used to support decision making and action taking

■ the predominant organizational culture.

_____

_____

_____

On reflection, would you say that the current mix of strategies being used to drive the business has been determined from a clear appreciation of the business idea? If not, then what would you see as their source?

_____

_____

_____

Has the mix and focus of the strategies been adapted to match changes in the business context? If not, then why do you think that this is so?

_____

_____

_____

Looking back over the past five years, identify six key business decisions that have been made. Against each of these make a note as to how they have influenced the current capability and performance of the business.

Figure 7.7 Key past decisions and their influence on current capability and performance

Decision	Influence on current capability and performance

Conventional wisdom suggests that the ability of a business to change direction is limited. The limitations are attributed to the patterns of decision making that have gone before. These decisions will have moved management thinking to a position that reflects this learning from the past. Where the business is established in an industry it will be following what is known as the "industry recipe." This notion of a business learning has been extended to the notion that organizations create and follow a definable trajectory. Most trajectories become stable and predictable. Incremental changes to these trajectories are possible, but a major or radical shift only occurs when a cataclysmic event is encountered, events typically associated with a takeover or a change of executive. Understanding the factors that restrict changes to the direction of a business is crucial to linking business development to successful implementation.

Past learning can be both a strength and a source of vulnerability. Your experiences will cause you to emphasize some aspects of the business context and ignore others. The mental models or schemas that you use to help make sense of complexity will be well developed. As you worked through the above review there were opportunities to change or reconsider the validity of these schemas. Our preparedness to learn decreases as we become more satisfied with past successes. Alternatively, when facing an apparent failure, the tendency is to move on and rationalize that we had merely experienced an anomaly. My recommendation is that you regularly review the schemas that you are using to make sense of the business context. Challenge the mental models and the underlying values you are using. In this way you will have grounded both your mental models and the problem being tackled in the reality of a world that is unfolding. Figure 7.8 shows how mental models need to be challenged.

Figure 7.8 Challenging mental models

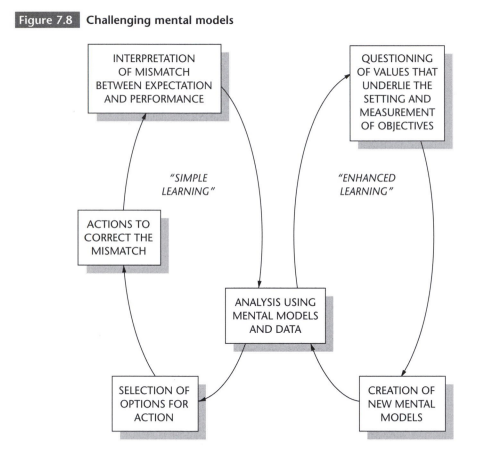

Adapted from an idea attributable to Argyris, C. and Schon, D. (1978) *Organizational Learning.*

SUMMARY

You have now completed the reviews that establish the foundation of the business development process. The breakthrough is having recognized the significance of understanding the business context. More importantly, you will have gained a clear understanding of the business idea that is being used to drive the business. You are now in a position to see how business logic, how you make sense of a business situation, forms the basis of thinking about business options and subsequent action This understanding is more difficult to achieve than at first sight it might appear. You will need to practice this until it becomes a part of your natural approach.

Your experiences of conducting business reviews and gathering data about the competition is, I expect, quite extensive. You may be thinking that there is a lot more to conducting and reviewing a business than answering the questions in the above section. This is not an uncommon feeling, but as you proceed with the book you will become much more adept at deciding how much information and investigation is required to make business decisions. Any one of the areas that are covered in a business review can be the subject of rigorous analysis and debate. But business management is not a precise science. There are no simple formula that if followed will result in achieving competitive advantage. We are on a quest to create the skills base and approaches that will enable you to read competitors' moves and at the same time make your play, being sufficiently adept at learning from observation to know when to make the next move.

The review of stakeholders highlighted the balancing act that business managers have to learn and perfect. Armed with a clear view of your mission and aspirations, this balancing act becomes more manageable. But throughout all of the above analysis and thinking you will have repeatedly found that you were relying on "best judgement". It is this personal judgement that I am helping you to develop through tackling these reviews. But a lot of the learning from experiences in dealing with business development issues will have to be unlearned. This is no bad thing, as a true learner is someone who recognizes the need to jettison the baggage that is no longer paying off. As you do this you will need to negotiate your changing perspectives and approach with colleagues. This takes us to our third skill, that of winning support for your strategies.

Part **3** B

Winning support
for your strategies

Chapter **8**

Influencing others

Using mental maps

The notion that we make sense of complexity by using mental maps is not new. Consultants and gurus come armed with their own maps and vie with each other in telling us how business really works. The forceful consultants, probably the ones that we listen to most readily, will be quite explicit about how we should interpret the business world. Michael Porter, Ansoff and a host of others are happy to give us their maps. It would be naïve to suggest that these maps serve no purpose. We all need to make sense of our complex worlds. The human condition drives us towards this quest for understanding. But here we are in pursuit of a set of skills that will enable us to create some original ways of making sense of business situations. We are trying to bring to the competitive business game a unique play that will defeat our opponents, or at least deliver our objectives.

Contemporary research suggests that our mental maps are stored at a subliminal level. That we store the data at this level and only construct clear maps when confronted with a need to make a decision. As a manager you are likely to spend a great deal of time trying to make your maps more explicit and share them with colleagues. How you set about doing this will be influenced by the first two skills that we have reviewed. Tackling the next review will reveal how effective you are at using mental maps to create new knowledge.

REVIEW 8

The two extreme metaphors used to describe an organization are the machine and the living organism. Make a note of a metaphor that could be used as a shorthand way of describing your organization.

_____

_____

_____

Make a list of the colleagues that you interface with when debating important issues. Indicate, against each, the metaphors that they would use to describe the organization.

_____

_____

_____

List the features of the current business direction over which your colleagues would agree and where you would expect disagreement.

_____

_____

_____

Based on findings from Review 5 on page 112, list three dominant strategies that are being pursued by the business. Against each of these make a note of the assumptions that you have made as to why they are key and how they will impact on business performance over the next three years.

Also note the level of agreement about each of the assumptions, that you would expect to get from your colleagues. Use Fig. 8.1, to capture your thoughts.

Figure 8.1 **Assumptions behind the key business strategies**

	Underlying assumptions (List three against each strategy.)	The anticipated level of agreement expected from colleagues (Show as high, medium or low.)	The anticipated impact of the strategy on business performance (Show as high, medium or low.)
Key strategy 1			
Key strategy 2			
Key strategy 3			

The hallmark of an effective business manager lies in the way they approach making sense of the uncertainty and ambiguity that surrounds how to develop the business. They use mental maps and explanatory frameworks to describe complex situations and incorporate hard or quantifiable data with the softer data that comes from their experiences and beliefs. Interpretation of any unique business opportunity then follows from this process. Figure 8.2 illustrates these parallel paths of analysis.

> **The hallmark of an effective business manager lies in the way they approach making sense of the uncertainty and ambiguity that surrounds how to develop the business**

Figure 8.2 Interpreting strategic opportunities

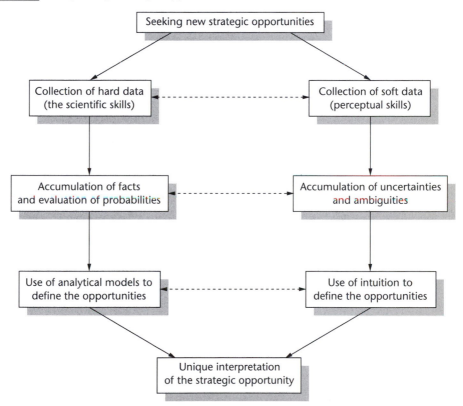

This process does not take place in isolation. To be effective we need to harness the collective knowledge and experiences of the business team. This is achieved by using frameworks or representations of the business complexity that encourages others to make statements about their assumptions and values. Your role now has to include that of the catalyst in three areas:

- helping to make explicit and change the mental models held by decision makers in the organization

- clarifying what is predictable and what is uncertain in the business environment

- introducing new perspectives to the decision makers based on a mixture of critical analysis and deep intuitive thinking.

Your reviews of the business idea, the business context, the business direction, and the dominant strategies being pursued, are based on the mental maps that drive your thinking. Not surprisingly your colleagues will be using their own maps. These will have been developed through solving the problems that arise in the process of running the business and making operational decisions. Creation of these maps and how they are used to expose our thinking takes place at a subliminal level. The reality in most organizations is that decisions about business development are made *on the hoof*. It is only when we reflect on where the business decisions have taken us, and where the longer-term future opportunities can be found, that we begin to reshape our mental maps. Learning becomes a reflective activity.

Dialogue

To help your colleagues engage in this reflective activity and reveal their mental maps, you need to employ the use of dialogue. With dialogue the aim is to avoid the temptation to put across a viewpoint and to rely on argument in order to win the point. Dialogue goes beyond conventional discussion aimed at solving problems. The purpose is to use dialogue to produce new knowledge by exposing and developing the mental maps held by colleagues. A great deal of the content of the maps that drive thinking is based on deeply held values that are often expressed in the form of opinions. Although we are all experts at expressing our opinions, we rarely expose the values on which they are based.

Dialogue goes beyond conventional discussion aimed at solving problems

Many of the features of these mental maps are based on knowledge that has accumulated over many years. Some of this knowledge will be held at the explicit level and much will be hidden or be held at a tacit level. Sharing this tacit knowledge is a vital step to creating new knowledge from the collective experiences and thinking of the team. Once the mental models have surfaced the challenge is to build a shared model of how to grow the business over the longer term. The model must then be tested for reality and relevance to the business. This requires that the team see each other as colleagues rather than adversaries who are trying to argue contrary views. The power of using dialogue, as opposed to conventional discussion and debate, is that new ways of thinking about, valuing and framing issues, are developed. But it would be naïve to assume that this takes place in a value-free environment. Some colleagues have more power than others and will be following what they see as a political agenda. In the next section we will explore how power and politics can be managed.

Handling power and politics

As an experienced manager you know how important it is to harness organizational power and manage local politics when dealing with operational issues. But where business issues are debated and key strategic decisions are being structured and made, then the game becomes much more complex. The traditional view of the primacy of the shareholder, who has to be satisfied, has been extended to recognize that there are a range of stakeholders in the business. Added to this, the notion of the Chief Executive acting as the agent in handling company affairs on behalf of the stakeholders has also been challenged. Executives are often shareholders and have a vested interest in how the affairs of the firm are conducted and in the medium- to short-term outcomes. The longer-term business direction and the decisions are clouded by this mix of interests. We saw in the previous section that the use of dialogue helps to surface some of the tacit thinking and value-driven positions that colleagues hold. But you will still be surrounded by colleagues who will be attempting to sell their ideas using whatever means are available. For many business managers this is what makes the game worth playing and it is argued that power and politics create the pressure from which winning approaches to growth evolve.

There are two notions that are central to detecting and influencing where and how power and politics are being used to influence business decisions. The first involves the use of rhetoric and the premise statement. The second concerns how organizational paradoxes are presented and argued. We will take a look at how these two devices are used and then give you an opportunity to see how they apply in your organization.

Rhetoric

The use of logic and deductive reasoning provides a powerful approach to developing an argument or promoting a point of view. When this fails then adopting a rhetorical style can often overcome any gaps and be used to sway an audience. With the rhetorical style you will find that a major premise is presented that masks the ambiguities and uncertainties surrounding a business issue. Once the premise is accepted then further minor premises are used to reach a conclusion. Where the premise is presented by a powerful and eloquent colleague then the premise will be hard to refute. I am not saying that it is wrong to use rhetoric and premise statements when arguing a position, but simply alerting you to the dangers that this approach presents to the quest to understand others. When trying to encourage colleagues to surface and question deeply held values, then persuasion is perhaps something that needs to be used sparingly. The skill lies in recognizing when rhetoric is being used as a persuasive device in order to close down options and knowing how to harness its strength.

Paradox

The second notion concerns how paradoxical statements are used in organizational language and thinking. Conventional approaches to managing organizations rely on eliminating differences and conflict. The power of that comes from using controls and motivational approaches to align staff around a common cause and this is a core management tenet. This alignment to a common cause leads to shared understanding, which in turn ensures that long-term decision making is executed with constancy and a clear purpose. But we know that this is rarely the case and that individuals interpret situations in a myriad of ways. These differences in interpretation create the richness and diversity within an organization that enables creativity to flourish. This presents us with a contradiction. On the one hand we want individuals to enjoy a shared meaning and an agreement on which actions are key to success. While on the other, we want them to pursue their own meaning and enjoy a sense of purpose that enables the organization to harness the unique talents and creativity of all. So we have an apparent contradiction on our hands. Do we seek to obtain a shared culture and set of meanings, or do we celebrate the differences? This can be represented as a paradox. A paradox is a statement that contains contradictory and apparently mutually exclusive propositions that are argued as being present as real phenomena, and being able to operate at the same time. There are many examples where paradoxes occur naturally in organizational activities:

- the drive for centralization of decision making and control, while knowing that decision making at the local level needs to be responsive to the interpretations of the local manager
- the desire to organize the work into divisions and separate groups, knowing that combinations and cross-fertilization of ideas and experiences enables firms to create superior performance
- the urgency to organize production to achieve lowest cost, while recognizing that the customer's perception of value added will probably demand higher quality and support, and hence higher manufacturing costs.

The list goes on, but the point being made is that by framing dichotomies in the form of paradoxes it is possible to establish where the power and politics in the organization reside. The review below will help you apply these two important notions.

The first part of this review invites you to build up a series of premise statements that are then used to create a rhetorical argument. Refer back to Review 6 on page 117 where you considered the current business direction, the key business decisions that have been taken and the mix of strategies that are being implemented. Assume that you are now being pressed by a key stakeholder group and that you want to persuade them that your views about how the business should be grown and developed are valid. Produce a simple sentence that would describe the key growth strategy that has been followed and whether it has worked.

_____

_____

_____

Produce a simple statement expressing an opportunity that you see for the business to pursue further growth.

_____

_____

_____

Produce a simple statement of the actions that have to be taken to seize this opportunity, i.e. the strategy that has to be followed and the strategic investment decisions that have to be made.

_____

_____

_____

Produce a simple statement of the outcomes that will result from taking these actions.

_____

_____

_____

Now read through the above statements and adjust the wording so that you have a plausible series of statements that represent a rhetorical argument for a new strategic direction for the business.

The second part of this review invites you to identify the key paradoxes that drive strategic thinking and decision making in your organization. The balance or extremes of position that you hold among these paradoxes gives a measure of the tension that organizational power and politics have created. We begin with an illustration of how a paradoxical statement is presented. The statement contains two apparently mutually exclusive ideas. Each of these ideas are in themselves perfectly viable when considered alone and would attract support. But supporting one of these ideas appears to challenge any support given to the other. For example:

We have become a large and complex organization and rely on the bureaucracy that we have developed to help keep track of things and maintain overall control. But as the competition seeks out our weak spots, we must ensure that while pursuing efficiency, we think and act like entrepreneurs at all levels of the business.

The paradox hidden in this statement is that of autonomy and control. It suggests that the organization wants the benefits that come from central control and conformity, while at the same time requiring that line managers act in independent ways, as though they were entrepreneurs. What I would like you to do is to study the list of paradoxical statements given below. Then use the grid (Fig. 8.3 overleaf) to indicate those paradoxes where you consider your opinion on how the business should be developed, structured and managed, would differ markedly from that held by the power group within the organization. What you are trying to do is to identify first the key paradoxes that are driving your organization and second where your views are at odds with those of the power-holders and influencers.

The paradox review

The position that you would take in arguing your view about the growth of your business can be shown by using Fig. 8.3 overleaf. Show also the position that would be taken by the power group or influencers in your organization. The following statements are given to illustrate how these paradoxes would be presented in a strategy meeting.

1. We must grant local autonomy while maintaining central control over key strategic areas.

2. We must create a strong culture and clear management processes while ensuring that we are open to new ideas and learning.

3. We must establish a clear set of plans and controls for growing the business, but at the same time recognize that flexibility will be required as the environment becomes more chaotic.

4. We must maintain and build on our current capabilities while at the same time seeking to break out of the tramlines in our strategic thinking.

5. The future success of the business will depend on the ability to institutionalize our knowledge, but we must also encourage the entrepreneurs who will create new thinking.

6. We want the divisions to compete as stand-alone businesses while recognizing that sharing knowledge and resources between the divisions will give us the synergies required for growth.

7. We must become the lowest cost producer while providing our customers with new, innovative and high quality products and services.

8. We will rely on growing through incremental improvements to existing products and services. But at the same time we must encourage the more breakthrough and radical innovations that will put us ahead of the competition.

9. By developing our core competences we will establish a competitive advantage, but by forming alliances and joint ventures with suppliers and customers we will be able to extend our competences beyond that of our own organization.

10. Short- and medium-term performance must dominate our business thinking, but those who are focused on the longer term must have an influence over the current business direction.

Figure 8.3 The paradox grid

		3	2	1	0	1	2	3	
1	Local autonomy								Central control
2	Strong culture								New learning
3	Conventional strategic management								Managing chaos
4	Encouraging new strategic thinking								Maintaining the status quo
5	Promoting the entrepreneurs								Institutionalizing knowledge through procedures and rules
6	Promoting competition between business divisions								Creating corporate synergies
7	Lowest cost producer								Innovation and high quality
8	Promoting radical innovation								Relying on incremental innovation
9	Securing and controlling in-house competences								Outsourcing through alliances and joint ventures
10	Short-term performance drives thinking								Long-term vision drives the current business thinking

COMMENTARY

Those who hold organizational power or are accepted in the role of the influencer will be masters of the use of rhetoric. It is a technique or skill that you need to practice. In the review you will have seen how it is possible to build up a series of statements that can be linked to make a convincing story.

Those who hold organizational power or are accepted in the role of the influencer will be masters of the use of rhetoric

The purpose of the rhetoric is to present an argument that appears to be logical, but is in fact a series of unproven premises. The intention is to make it impossible for the other party to present a counter-argument. I have given an example below that shows how the argument is developed. Compare this to your own review.

An example of rhetoric

1. Presentation of antecedents and the subsequent events that have arisen.
   By focusing entirely on our global branding strategies over the past five years, we have allowed our local competitors to capture our traditional home markets.

2. Presentation of objectives and performance.
   We set out to achieve world leadership and rapid growth. These have not been achieved.

3. Presentation of where the blame for failure must be placed.
   The marketing department and their relentless pursuit of global brand strategies opened the door for local competition who offered the home customers products with a wide range of functions and features. They attacked our home base with a differentiation strategy.

4. Presenting the cause of the failure and the effect.
   This decline in our home market share cut off the cash flows and profitability that we had historically relied on for investment and growth. Our circle of success has been broken.

5. Presentation of a way forward.
   We can recover if we stop investing in brand strategies and focus on product differentiation.

6. Presenting the outcomes of this strategy.
   We will secure strong home sales and the ability to feed our overseas markets with a range of competitive products that will capitalize on local variations in taste. We will regain our position as an innovative and forward thinking company. The economies of scale gained from these expanding markets will ensure the cash flows and profitability levels that are essential to the future expansion of the business.

Being aware of when this approach is being used gives you the opportunity either to challenge some of the premise statements or to decide if the particular battle is worth fighting. Those who over-play this approach are soon recognized and unless they are in an organizational power position, are likely to be marginalized. Many of the business issues that you will be tackling will not come surrounded by logical argument and hard facts. This encourages the use of rhetoric, and if you decide to use this device then make sure that your arguments are consistent with the standards of personal integrity that you have set yourself.

Use of paradox

With the use of the paradoxical statement you are trying to help uncover the reasoning that colleagues are using to support their arguments. The review of the key organizational paradoxes will have shown where the views that you hold are at variance with those of the power group and influencers. Discussion around these organizational dichotomies can be used to establish a level of tension from which the operational action and strategic direction are derived. The tension establishes an environment in which original thinking is generated and unique outcomes created. To do this effectively you need to adopt the following three rules.

1. Resist seeing the paradoxes as presenting you with a dilemma. You do not have to fight your corner and make choices.

2. Avoid the temptation to smooth out and blur the differences that colleagues have raised through the paradox.

3. Seek to understand the extremes that are being presented. Then engage in dialogue, as opposed to an argument, in order to see how the paradoxes might appear to have a different balance point or emphasis at strategic, operational or lower levels in the organization. The paradoxes may also be seen to change their balance over time as the organization develops and grows. For example, adopting an entrepreneurial approach during the introductory stages of a new business is appropriate. But as the business becomes established then a shift towards an approach that offers greater management control is more prudent.

By using a mixture of rhetoric and paradoxical statements you will be in a position to identify and influence the power groups in the organization. They are devices that are best used when the power figures signal a move from defensive to more combative positions. Surfacing a clear paradox will capture the attention of your colleagues and give you the opportunity to present and champion both extremes. But much of your success at achieving a major shift of thinking among colleagues will depend on your use of the predominant organizational culture. In the next section I will show you how this can be achieved.

Handling the culture and your impact on others

The notion that organizations have distinctive cultures is well established in management thinking. We talk about colleagues sharing a set of philosophies and common values. We believe that in a strong culture there is a clear understanding of how the organization works, how people expect to be treated, and how the organization manages itself in the external world. Identifying these norms of behavior is relatively easy, as their reality is substantiated through stories of success and failures plus the details of the sanctions and reward process. Recruitment rituals, organizational structures and titles all help to maintain the norms of behavior that identify the culture. This notion is very powerful and hence vital to those wishing to shape social constructions.

Cultures develop over time and critical incidents in the history of the organization have a major formative effect. Where the response to an incident is seen as successful in terms of reducing the risk to the organization or leading to some obvious benefits, then the response will be institutionalized. Stories quickly develop around what really created the success. The organization begins to see itself as having a reality and being a powerful force. Over a period of time these critical incidents are used to:

- demonstrate organizational values
- indicate what constitutes effective behavior
- show where authority resides
- signal what constitutes expertise
- confirm the role that the organization plays in the industry.

But there are dangers associated with an organization having a strong culture. The primary concern arises where the outcome of a decision or strategy is only partially successful. The temptation, where a strong culture exists, is to see the failure as an anomaly or, worse, as insignificant. The organizational response is therefore minimal and the management persist with the use of ingrained approaches. To an outsider the failure to take account of the anomaly is much more obvious. The organization has effectively institutionalized behavior that discounts marginal failures. It is only the more obvious failures that come under a process of critical review. Over a period of time, changes to the culture that can impact on organizational behavior become more difficult to achieve. Here we have a clear paradox. On the one hand we can see the need to establish a strong and shared culture as a means of ensuring consistent and predictable behaviors, but at the same time we want people to be open minded and able to respond to events in original ways. The next review will help you to identify the culture that is driving your business and discover how it can be used to influence business direction.

What metaphors would you use to:

■ capture a mental image of the prevailing culture in your organization?

_____

■ caricature how managers have to behave if they are to be seen as successful?

_____

■ describe the main power group?

_____

■ describe the rewards and sanctions processes?

_____

■ describe the organizational structure?

_____

Construct a statement that you would use to answer a newly recruited senior manager in your organization who asks: "What it is really like around here?" Make it a statement that captures what you believe represents the culture in terms of the norms of behavior and what being a part of the organization really means, i.e. the organizational paradigm.

_____

_____

_____

What are the key incidents that have shaped your organization over the past five years?

_____

_____

_____

Who are the key figures, in the recent history of the organization, that have shaped the current business direction?

_____

_____

_____

In the past five years, what attempts have been made to change the dominant organizational culture and were these attempts successful?

_____

_____

_____

Indicate, in terms of high, medium and low, the extent to which you consider the current organizational culture is appropriate for influencing and building business relationships with the following groups:

- shareholders
- investment groups
- the Board
- industry bodies
- Government departments
- suppliers
- customers
- alliance partners.

Reflect on Review 6, where you gave your view of the future direction the business should take. This may involve changes to the current business idea, a refocus of strategies, changes to investment policies, reorganization, etc. Do you consider that the current organizational culture will sustain and support this future direction? If so, then in what ways does it provide this support? If not, then describe the features of the culture that has to be established. Record your views by answering the following questions.

How does the current organizational paradigm support your vision of the future direction for the business?

_____

_____

_____

If you consider that the current organizational paradigm has to change, what would the new paradigm be?

_____

_____

_____

In this review you saw how important it is to be able to identify the prevailing organizational culture and understand how it has been created and how it is being sustained. In many organizations there will be more than one culture. At a corporate level it is likely that working on ambiguous and uncertain issues will have established a unique way of approaching decision making. At a business and divisional level the variety of shared experiences and the differing nature of external relationships will have created a range of dominant paradigms. But in all organizations there are six key factors that have a major impact on the formation of the organizational culture. These are as follows.

Six key factors affecting organizational culture

1. Social integration.

2. Personality and learning from previous cultures.

3. Developing defensive approaches – where individuals and groups learn how to hide the thinking behind key ideas.

4. Critical incidents – the use of rationalization on historic events in order to develop best practice for the group.

5. Impact of the founders and key leaders.

6. Impact of the reward systems.

If you decide that the culture has to be changed to support a new business idea or a refocusing of the dominant strategies, it is important to understand how culture is used.

How culture is used
The culture provides two basic functions for a group. First, it enables the group to manage the external environment, and second, to manage their internal affairs. The group will rely on the cohesiveness of the culture to reach:

- a shared understanding of the primary task of the group and the main functions that have to be carried out
- agreement on the atmosphere and climate within the group
- agreement on the primary goals
- agreement on how resources and expertise are to be utilized
- clarity as to how success and achievement are to be measured and the value that will be attributed to these measures.

The culture will also either support or threaten the promotion of critical debate, learning and creativity that are essential to the effective performance of the group. A final area where the group culture will have an impact is that of managing interfaces to external groups and the wider environment. This will include a range of stakeholders.

Changes to the culture

There is a great deal of advice available on how to design and manage changes to the organizational culture. We need to review some of the more successful practices. The most effective method is one where the Chief Executive identifies and promotes a vision of the future that stretches and inspires organizational members. A raft of approaches to implementation then follow, all of which aim to impact on the features of the existing culture that have been attributed to having caused the current malaise. The key here is to adopt an approach that emphasizes:

- changing the behavior rather than the underlying perceptions and mental models. This is appropriate where the required change is simply dependent on changes in behavior. This can then be sustained through the use of sanctions and rewards
- making a more creative use of the existing culture. This can be useful where a re-orientation to how the groups perceive themselves will provide the required change in behavior.

For many managers, conducting a review of the organizational culture is very difficult. Personal involvement and identification with the events and colleagues make it easy to overlook areas where the culture has become a block to progress. The very fact that cultures are used to protect and provide comfort for the inmates means that they become a strong filter through which we view a potentially hostile world. But the culture does represent our social constructions, both internal and external to the organization. To make use of and master this area requires a fine balance between over-introspection and a level of objectivity. It is vital to recognize where the culture is out of step with the changing environment. In the next section we will explore how leadership skills can be used to influence colleagues within the culture.

Tapping into your natural leadership

The notion of leadership fascinates and at the same time confuses the experienced manager. Hopefully most of the myths that derive from arguments about being a born leader, the part that personality plays, and the effectiveness of different styles have been adequately covered by films, fiction writers and exposure to life. But in order to harness this notion of leadership and link it to the influencing process then we need to look closely at how it works.

The leader as task manager

Leadership is about how to manage organizations. At one level we will find ourselves holding an organizational position that carries with it the formal responsibility for achieving a complex task with a set of resources. At another level we could be engaged as a facilitator in helping a group make sense of an ambiguous and uncertain set of conditions. You will have had a lot of experience with the former role. Here the expectation is that as the leader you set the direction, acting as a visionary and designer in helping staff undertake a complex task. In the conventional top down approach to developing a business we would expect that:

- the corporate group or chief executive would set the long-term goals

- plans are then generated to match the organization's internal resources to the external threats and opportunities, monitoring and control being a major issue

- an organizational culture and style are designed to match the needs of the external environment and be conducive to the motivation and control of staff.

- organizational structures are set up to mirror the business strategies.

Many organizations work on the basis that this task-focused orientation is the best approach. In general terms I would agree. Where people are engaged in group processes then they seek and expect the leader to find some way of helping them to work together effectively. They are willing to accept direction and where there is a need to face up to difficult trade-offs they expect the leader to make the right decisions. Once the formal groups have been established then a vast network of informal relationships will form. The purpose and focus of some of these relationships will be to detract from the primary task. To ensure that these informal groups do not subvert the primary task, the leader uses the attractiveness of the organizational vision and the homogeneity of the culture to keep them focused on the desired behavior and outcomes.

The leader as facilitator

Alternatively, the leader as facilitator is a role that is well recognized but extremely difficult to play. Discovery and experimentation are encouraged. Individuals are empowered in such a way that creativity and risk taking become a group norm. In this role the leader establishes the following business development process:

- small disturbances or anomalies in the business operation are highlighted
- individuals and groups then amplify the possible significance of these anomalies and seek political support for their views
- traditional mental models are brought into question by these anomalies and conversational dialogue is used to test out their relevance to the organization
- the power in political alliances, judgements over external pressures and intuition are then used to determine the timing and extent of any action
- new mental models, frames of reference and ways of working are established and institutionalized.

Adopting a role

The extent to which you adopt either of these roles will, of course, depend on the context in which the business is operating and the pressures which you determine are the ones that have to be addressed. Where you are in a position of authority and the business direction is quite clear, then a task focus is appropriate. Your skills of persuasion and influence are then used to build relationships and communicate the corporate purpose. Where your authority is much less clear, your influence will depend on your skills in agenda setting and encouraging staff to identify and manage anomalies. With this background you need to focus on your own approaches and abilities in harnessing leadership as part of the influencing process.

REVIEW 11

Reflect back to Review 10 on page 144, where you identified the dominant organizational paradigm that supports your business. To what extent do you consider that you have flexibility in how you play your leadership role within that paradigm? Make notes on the areas where the role is constrained and where there is total freedom.

_____

_____

_____

During the past five years, what were the two major successes and the two major failures that you have been associated with in the business? Identify against each the dominant leadership role that you were playing. Use Fig. 8.4 to record these reflections.

Figure 8.4 Success and the leadership role

	Visionary, direction setter, designer, authority figure	Facilitator, agenda setter, process manager
Major success 1		
Major success 2		
Major failure 1		
Major failure 2		

What metaphor would capture the leadership style that you find most natural to adopt?

_____

_____

_____

What pressures *outside* the organization have the greatest influence on the leadership style that you are currently adopting?

_____

_____

_____

What pressures *inside* the organization have the greatest influence on the leadership style that you are currently adopting?

_____

_____

_____

The following lists describe the characteristics of four leadership styles. Consider these and then decide which most closely fits the style that you feel comfortable with. Use Fig. 8.5 overleaf to record your findings.

Style A

Operating in the present, emphasizing the immediacy of matters.

Seen as in charge of the situation.

Demanding high performance from staff.

Holding strong views as to the action that has to be taken.

Valuing some staff more highly than others.

Style B

Helping the team to share ideas.

Identifying closely with staff.

Wanting to get to the heart of any conflict among staff.

Determined to please everyone.

Minimizing the use of personal or positional power.

Style C

Never seen to be critical or judgemental.

Very supportive to subordinates.

Not highlighting mistakes made by staff.

Sensitive and responsive to the moods of staff.

Non directive.

Constantly praising staff.

Avoiding confrontation.

Style D

Supportive of the organizational rules and procedures.

Focusing on routine activities.

Avoiding tackling open-ended issues.

Playing down the value of the informal group.

Being seen as unemotional.

Being seen as preferring to work alone.

Figure 8.5 Leadership style audit

	Close match	Occasional match	Rare match
Style A			
Style B			
Style C			
Style D			

There are a number of ways in which you can influence the operational and strategic activities of the organization. Use Fig. 8.6 to indicate which you currently use and the area of influence.

Figure 8.6 Influencing operational and strategic activities

	Influence over operational activities	Influence over strategic activities
Through organizational position		
By being a member of the power group		
By virtue of functional expertise and experience		
By being a member of a key management process		
By influencing the organizational agenda		
By being valued by the operational managers		
By being valued by those setting the strategic direction		
By involvement in strategic decision making		
By dint of personality and charisma		
By being valued as having excellent intuition and insight		

The ability to influence the processes and decisions in operational and strategic areas in an organization are closely linked to relationships that you have established outside the organization. Use Fig. 8.7 to identify the areas and links that you utilize when seeking support.

Figure 8.7 Links used to gain leadership and support

	Influence over operational activities	Influence over strategic activities
Links to major stakeholder groups		
Links to the industry standard setting groups		
Links to suppliers		
Links to key customers and groups		
Links to key competitors		
Links to Trades Unions		
Links to Government		
Links to professional groups		
Other links		

COMMENTARY

This review presented you with a challenge. It is easy to decide on the leadership role to adopt in a particular set of circumstances. But application is quite another matter. As a busy manager you handle a myriad of situations each day and given sufficient time you could work out the appropriate role. But this is rarely the case and you find yourself falling back on to habitual approaches. By asking you to reflect on past successes and failures I wanted you to see the importance of deciding when it is vital to take the time to consider the role and style that should be adopted. The visionary and authority figure when the task is relatively clear, and the more facilitative role when exploration is the best approach to handling complexity. Your selection of an appropriate metaphor to capture your style will have given you an insight into where your influencing ability needs to be developed. Obviously both internal and external organizational pressures will have an impact on both your role and style when faced with leadership issues. The tendency is to focus on internal pressures as these are more immediate and obvious. But you also need to look outside the organization for the sources of pressure on business performance and your leadership style.

Leadership styles

In analyzing your style you will have seen how the emphasis moves between two extremes. A focus on the structure of the task in hand or on the interpersonal relationships that you form with colleagues and staff. The extent to which you adopt these two extremes will depend on how you interpret the pressure that you are working under. Under normal conditions you may exhibit style "B" but under stress move rapidly to Style "A." The style that you adopt will also be influenced by:

- your personality

- the pressures that your staff and colleagues place upon you

- your interpretation of the demands of the task and your ability to satisfy these demands

- your interpretation of the constraints and boundaries created by the organization

- the cultural values and expectations within the organization

- your personal, positional and expertise power

- the response that you get from staff and colleagues to the role that you adopt and the style that you exhibit.

Each style has its own characteristics and the significance that this has on your ability to harness leadership must not be underestimated.

Style A: Here the task dominates your behavior. Your fear of failure at the task and subsequent loss of power and influence become the driving motivational force. Under normal conditions this style will mark you as being directive but fair. But under pressure you are likely to revert to an autocratic style. The danger arises when this style reduces the opportunities for you to form coalitions and reach a compromise when faced with a conflict or dilemma. This style is highly prized in organizations where implementation of clear policies and decisions are involved. It is less effective where the issues are ambiguous and uncertain.

Style B: Your efforts here are to link your staff and colleagues to the task in hand. A leader who adopts this role is often seeking self-fulfilment and wants all staff to be satisfied with their situation. This style works well and highly informed and motivated staff complete work to schedule. But under pressure the leader will compromise over the demands of the task in order to avoid staff dissatisfaction over key decision areas of their work.

Style C: This style indicates that the leader values relationships with staff and colleagues more than the task in hand. Fear of disapproval from the team and rejection are the driving forces here. Staff detect a lack of direction from the leader and the focus on personal loyalty as a prerequisite to group member-ship leads to the group becoming isolated from the rest of the organization. Once again the danger is that under pressure the leader becomes an idealist at the expense of the task.

Style D: This style relies heavily on the use of logical and rational methods of working. The leader makes extensive use of rules and procedures to manage both the task and the staff. The focus is on survival in an uncertain world. By not becoming involved with staff the leader avoids dependency and having to face and deal with uncertainties. Under pressure the leader relies more and more on the protection provided by the organizational rules and processes.

Your power to influence

The final area in the review focused on your ability to influence operational and strategic activities in the organization. There are many arenas in which you can develop and exercise your ability to influence the thinking and actions of colleagues. The most obvious of these is to play in the arena fre-quented by the power group and dominant coalitions. But there are others where the agenda is set and key political support can be gained. A typical example is where the organization establishes key investigatory and decision-making processes. These include processes such as:

- strategic direction setting and review

- environmental scanning

- business development and planning

- operations development and planning

- investment planning

- project planning and management

- quality and standard setting

- business control, reporting and reviewing

- new product development and corporate venturing.

Participation in these processes provides opportunities to exert influence and enhance your standing both within and outside the organization. Ensuring that your presence is recognized and valued requires constant attention to key relationships. It is all too easy for people to take you for granted and to pigeon-hole your talents and contributions. Keeping a check on your network of relationships and how you are valued by the key players is a skill that the influencer has to acquire. This will enable you to be connected to and able to seize opportunities to harness your leadership and influencing abilities. That brings us to the final area of the influencing process, that of gaining recognition.

Gaining recognition

To succeed in the workplace you need to be in a position where your views are not only heard but can influence the way colleagues think and act. The extent to which we are heard depends on how closely the concepts being discussed are similar in the minds of both parties. For example, when presenting a viewpoint about the need to take account of an event happening outside the business, your audience will be judging the efficacy of your statements from two standpoints. The extent to which they:

- have previously met with success when following your advice in similar situations
- value your ability as a collector, analyst and presenter of information.

Discrepancies in the communication will be debated and some consensus on meanings finally reached. But your ultimate success in influencing the audience depends on how much added value they will derive from accepting any subsequent transactions. Put simply, they want to know what is in it for themselves. Your views and proposals also need to be seen by colleagues as credible. They will be considering the extent to which they can believe in what you are saying and, where a transaction is involved, the extent to which your message is wholly truthful and not biased to give you an advantage and them a loss. There is a natural tendency to believe someone when it is obviously in their self interest to be telling what is, to the best of their knowledge, the truth. This tends to be more the case where the relationship has not been truly established. With close colleagues and confidants then the communication and transaction processes are much more open and trusting.

Integrity

A strong and clear display of integrity is essential to gaining recognition. It takes a long time to be accepted as someone who has integrity and one slip can immediately undo years of honest dealings. This is an area where perseverance and risk taking will eventually establish your position as someone whose word can be trusted. Those with whom you usually agree will trust you automatically. We all have a tendency to believe those who agree with us because we assume that their judgement must be the same as ours. The danger of this approach is to fail to recognize that colleagues will be responding to us in a similar way. They maintain their credibility with us by agreeing with our judgements and conclusions. They will be loud with their agreements and keep their disagreements at a low level. Interpreting ready acceptance of our proposals and ideas as an agreement is not a wise path to tread. Neither should we conclude that our audience have no strong views of their own.

Good listening

Being heard is obviously important, but so is listening. Most of us consider that we are good listeners, but being an active listener is a habit that we need to acquire. We are all able to spot the colleague who is making lots of sounds that suggest we have their full attention. But the true listener is the person who challenges what we have said in order to elicit a full understanding of our meaning. In business this is incredibly important, even when faced with a hostile audience. Getting behind their hostility to the reasons and values that are creating the rejection, is an important habit to develop. Hostile audiences, as well as tried and trusted friends, want to be understood, and have their views affirmed and appreciated. Putting yourself in the position of the audience and seeing your proposition from their viewpoint as well as your own is a salutary but essential process that you have to practice. It may mean making yourself vulnerable to criticism and having to modify your proposition. After all, it is the audience that you want to persuade and empathize with. Your use of logic and reasoning becomes much more effective when it is based on a balance between your integrity, ability to empathize, and to present a logical argument. If you reflect for a moment on the approach you have developed when presenting a proposition, the above order is usually reversed. You start with a logical argument and then prepare yourself to fight off any disagreements and objections. The byword that you need to adopt is one of seeking a win for both sides rather than the conventional one of "I win and you lose." Having established the background, I want you to conduct a review of how you set out to gain recognition among colleagues.

REVIEW 12

Use Fig. 8.8 overleaf to rank your personal credibility, in terms of high, medium and low, as seen by the various groups.

Figure 8.8 Auditing your expertise and credibility

Area of expertise and credibility	The power group	Your team	Other colleagues	Key groups outside the organization
Technology				
Marketing				
Financial				
Operational				
Industry				
Using internal networks				
Using external networks				

Think back to the last time you presented a proposal that involved a significant change to either the operation of the business or the strategic direction. Make a brief note about the key features of the proposal and the impact that you anticipated that it would have on the audience.

_____

_____

_____

Use your reflections and the above statement to answer the following questions.

- What personal characteristic did you feel was most likely to work in favor of your proposal being heard and understood?
- How confident were you as to your personal credibility with that audience?
- What evidence did you use to judge your credibility with that audience?

■ To what extent were you attempting to win, in getting your proposal accepted, and what personal benefits were attached to this acceptance?

_____

_____

_____

COMMENTARY

This review highlighted one of the most sensitive areas in your personal development. It is never easy to be totally open and self-critical, or self-congratulatory, when reflecting on how you set about gaining recognition and acceptance. This goes far beyond the notion of being liked. Being a likeable fool or a likeable rascal has little to do with your quest to develop effective strategic behavior. Here we are concerned with personal credibility that is founded on a demonstration of integrity and an ability to offer expertise and sound guidance to colleagues facing complex operational and strategic issues.

The review of the areas in which your expertise and credibility are recognized by various groups may have given you a few surprises. It is unreasonable to expect to have scored a high rating in more than two or three areas. But it is important to note where your rating was high with one group and low with another when considering the same area of expertise. This will show you where your current approach needs reviewing and developing. Gaining recognition is dependent on a mixture of personal characteristics, feelings of self worth and an ability to understand what frames of reference and values are being used by your audience. The temptation to see and prepare for every briefing or presentation of a proposal as though it is a competition is always with us.

SUMMARY

You have now completed a review of the five areas that underpin the skill of influencing others. We saw how the assumptions surrounding our thinking about business development have to be shared with colleagues if we want their commitment. By negotiating any differences in perception, agreement can be reached on areas of risk surrounding key business decisions. We also saw that business development is often carried out at operational levels in the organization and that the mental models used for longer-term business thinking are quite different from those used to determine short-term actions. If we are to help colleagues to surface the mental models that drive their views of the future direction of the business, then dialogue holds the key to success. An approach that runs counter to the natural tendency to seek to argue and win our point.

▶

▶ Review 8 highlighted the difficulty faced when communicating to colleagues deeply-held views on key business decisions. Thankfully, organizations are not value-free debating chambers. The pressure to satisfy a range of stakeholders, some of whom hold very vested interests in the business, is a key determinant in any attempt at persuasion. The technique of using rhetoric to present and win an argument was contrasted with the more subtle use of the organizational paradox. The review of key organizational paradoxes may have provided some surprises. The paradox is a simple device of language and yet managers find themselves constantly dissipating time and energy attempting to win debates over the emphasis in a paradox rather than harnessing the power that it contains.

The power that can be gained from utilizing the organizational culture was shown in Review 10. In most organizations conformity to a set of behaviors is often sufficient for the effective running of the business. But for some, a deeper commitment to a set of values and beliefs may be essential. The decision as to which level you need to reach will depend on the context and your position in the organization. Once again we saw how metaphor can be used to probe colleagues' perceptions about the organizational culture. Reviewing key events and identifying the main players in the history of the business gave a good insight into how the culture had been established and was being maintained. Armed with an ability to recognize the organizational paradigm you are in a good position to consider how it supports the current business direction. This matching between the culture and the business direction is one of the key outcomes of this review. Changing the culture, where a mismatch is seen, needs to be approached with caution. The advice is that unless faced with a dramatic need to change the direction and focus of the business, it is better to harness the existing culture rather than setting out to create a new one.

The leadership position brings with it an ideal opportunity to influence others. But being clear about the role that best fits the situation needs careful consideration. Ingrained approaches and personal motivation play a big part in determining how we behave as a leader. There are pressures from staff, colleagues and parties outside the organization, demanding a response to their wants and needs. Developing the habit of recognizing and balancing these pressures will help your leadership role. We also saw that there are many arenas in which you can practice your leadership skills even when not in an organizationally defined position of power. By considering these arenas, from investment planning to corporate venturing processes, you will quickly widen your sphere of influence.

Gaining recognition relies heavily on your ability to be seen as credible by your audience. Credibility is closely linked to integrity and steadfastness of purpose. You need to be recognized as offering your audience an area of expertise that they can value, one that provides them with benefits and no losses. We also saw that your credibility will vary between groups. Gaining recognition is a vital step in influencing others and is something that the busy manager often takes for granted. But these generic skills are played out in specific, not general, contexts. This takes us to the fourth skill, that of taking action in context.

Chapter **9**

Taking action in context

Balancing the stakeholders

It will come as no surprise to hear that the owners of a business expect a financial return on their investment. But there are two distinct views held on ownership of a business. One where the assets are deployed by the owners and the other where there is only a traceable responsibility for the outcome arising over the use of the assets. The legal form of contract applies to the former and the later emphasizes the part played by the executives employed by the owners. In business there is a distinction made between the reward and risk that comes from direct ownership and that arising from being an agent of the owners.

Share ownership is increasingly used as a means of closing the motivational gap between the owners and the agents. This applies to Board members, both executive and non executive, as well as managers and staff. Share ownership has become increasingly important as a means of balancing this spread of interest. What we are touching on here is the split between ownership and control. In many businesses the owner and the equity investors are increasingly only able to exercise power through a chain of agents and intermediaries. In developed nations the State is also able to act as the third hand in applying controls on businesses through legislation and regulatory bodies. The investors receive protection by these means but also find their control diminished. Attempting to balance these interests creates tensions at all levels in the business. The investors feel powerless; the corporate staff find themselves torn between short-term performance and long-term investment strategies; business managers focus on delivering on short-term financial returns. Meanwhile the wider public turn to governments and legislation to protect their interests from what they see as the deleterious effects of commercial corporations. At a higher level, Western governments struggle to produce guidelines and introduce policies that will direct company law regarding the duties of directors and the rights of shareholders and employees, the overall aim being to create transparency and co-operation between investors, firms and the State.

Your experiences will have exposed you to a range of business issues where conflicting stakeholder interests were involved. Your own interests will also have had an impact on how you interpreted those issues and the possible outcomes. The next review will show you how to tackle this balancing act and where your approach needs to be reviewed and developed.

REVIEW 13

Reflect on Review 5 on page 112, where you identified the business idea and how it is used to create added value for the customer and how the business direction has evolved. Then answer the following questions concerning the external and internal stakeholders in the business.

External stakeholders

- Who provides the finance for major long-term investment?
- Who provides the finance for medium-term projects?
- Who agrees the sources of funding used to finance the business operations?
- Identify any other external groups that influence long-term, medium-term and operational financing of the business.

- Who are the major clients, customers or users of the outputs of the business?
- Who are the major subcontractors used by the business?
- Who are the major suppliers of goods and services to the business?
- Who are the major alliance or joint venture partners?
- Who are the major competitors?

Internal stakeholders

- Who are the individuals or dominant power group that make long-term investment decisions?
- Who are the individuals or dominant power group that make medium-term decisions?

■ Who are the individuals or group that make tactical and operational decisions?

_____

_____

_____

Use Fig. 9.1 to synthesize the outcomes of the above analysis indicating the area of influence of each stakeholder and your view of the extent to which their interests are being satisfied.

Figure 9.1 **Stakeholders and their influence on decision making**

	Area of influence	High level of satisfaction	Medium level of satisfaction	Low level of satisfaction
External group				
Internal group				

Reflect on an occasion or event in the past year where you were involved in a decision process involving a trade-off between internal stakeholders. Note the details of this trade-off and comment on the following.

■ Were the conditions of the trade-off made clear to all parties?

■ Were all parties involved in the process and was it explicit?

■ What reactions were there from the parties that lost out on the trade-off decision?

_____

_____

_____

Repeat this review but this time consider an event that involved external stake-holders in the trade-off decision.

■ Were the conditions of the trade-off made clear to all parties?

■ Were all parties involved in the process and was it explicit?

■ What reactions were there from the parties that lost out on the trade-off decision?

_____

_____

_____

REVIEW 14

The following review explores your position regarding the need for a business to demonstrate a level of social responsibility. Business enterprises are encouraged to demonstrate what has been coined as their having a "social responsibility." their duties to society as a whole. Produce such a statement for your business.

_____

_____

_____

Use this statement to reflect on the trade-offs that you identified in the Review 14. What evidence is there that this "social responsibility" was applied to the external and internal trade-off decisions?

_____

_____

_____

Reflect back to Review 10 on page 144, where you looked at the key figures who have had the greatest influence on shaping and determining the strategic direction of the business.

What aspect of the "social responsibility" statement made above, was driving their thinking and actions?

_____

_____

_____

To what extent do you consider that the personal goals that you identified in Review 1, are in tune with the declaration of "social responsibility" that is currently being made by your company?

_____

_____

COMMENTARY

Your review of the stakeholders and what motivates or drives their interests will have been made from what is described as an "instrumentalist perspective." This perspective assumes that it is possible to identify the various interest groups and then work out the best way of balancing their demands and potential contribution to the business. The objective is to minimize interference while gaining their support in order to maximize the business interests. Taking such an approach may sound extreme. But vested self interest sounds a bit more excusable when considered from the point of view that all the stakeholders will be adopting the "I win and you lose" approach. Pressure from the stakeholders involves making trade-offs or choices among competing interests. These choices are based on beliefs as to the overall purpose of the organization and vested interests. The temptation is to assume that there is shared agreement over the organizational purpose and the stakeholder interests. The point here is that organizations interact with and rely on a very wide set of interest groups. To assume that decisions can be taken in a vacuum and weighed against simple criteria would be naïve.

Shareholders

The initial section of Review 13 enabled you to identify the sources of external funding and the groups that have the greatest influence on the share price and image of the organization in the financial marketplace. Some shareholders or investment groups expect the firm to produce short-term profits and pay an attractive dividend, whereas others are more interested in the longer-term value of their investment as gauged by, for example, the price to earnings ratio. This shareholder value perspective is very deeply ingrained at the executive level in organizations and is often the main criteria used for an investment or budgeting decision. But there is less agreement on the best way to generate shareholder value. Arguments range from those who see the Chief Executive being responsible for managing the long-term investment risks to those who see the shareholder as the decision maker – deciding on the amount and timing of the risks that they are prepared to take with their capital. One of the difficulties faced by the shareholders is to decide just what level of risk they are facing. But if one believes that the shareholder is in the decision-making position then it is the responsibility of the business managers, as their agents, to provide clear information so that shareholders can evaluate risk and manage their investment portfolio. This concern, over the notion of ownership of an enterprise, has spawned an extended debate around what is termed "corporate governance."

Many executives still support the belief that the purpose of the enterprise is to support the shareholders and not to champion the interests of a wider group of stakeholders. The view taken is that negotiations carried out with these stakeholder groups should be aimed at safeguarding the fundamental interests of the shareholders. The argument is that institutions and groups outside the firm should be set up to address and safeguard the interests of these other stakeholders and that while their interests are important to the survival and well-being of the enterprise, they are not its responsibility. Your review of stakeholder interests and their potential contributions to the organization will have highlighted these points and my purpose in doing this was to help you decide just how extreme a position you were taking regarding ownership and distribution of wealth.

Balancing interests of internal and external stakeholders

It is also important to understand the arguments over the need to balance the interests of external stakeholders with those of stakeholders inside the organization. All these groups are partners in the wider enterprise and the success of all the partners depends on co-operation and mutual support. Any bias or unfair trade-offs are seen as unjust or, at worst, immoral. Your review of the internal stakeholders and their interests will have highlighted how fragile these relationships are in practice. This will have been particularly evident from your reviews of the negotiation and decision-making processes that have affected the business.

The question of there being a higher level of social responsibility, to which those in a business should give their support, was raised. You may have found that this was quite a tall order when you considered the difficulty that you face in making your own feelings and values explicit when working with your colleagues. It is more a question of knowing that there are conflicting perspectives about ownership that are used in making business decisions rather than having to take a position. You need to be able to recognize when these perspectives are being brought into play and persuade colleagues to debate ownership issues. The issue of social responsibility is not an everyday topic in business. But it is important that you are able to present your views to colleagues. Particularly where you find that the values being used in business decisions do not align with those that form part of your longer-term vision. This takes us to our next area of action taking in context, that of how to apply controls to the business development process and evaluate the outcomes.

The issue of social responsibility is not an everyday topic in business

Is it sensible to try to control performance?

In business your effectiveness in taking action and deciding what outcomes are to be given priority depends a great deal on your motives and power position. For example, the head of a conglomerate, the darling of the investment world in the 1980s, would have unashamedly focused on acquisition of businesses. The purpose of the acquisitions would have been to add to the total value of the parent body. Value in this instance being measured in terms of capitalization of share value and growth of the asset base. The acquired business would usually be in a mature industry and the potential value would either be in the subsequent sale of undervalued assets or in gaining increased profitability margins through tight management controls. In contrast the head of a multinational would be seeking acquisitions that would add to the core business, provide access to an extended marketplace or to create synergies that supported the activities of the core business. These corporate-level decisions are always presented as being strategic rather than concerned with simple accounting gain and short-term profitability. When viewed from this corporate perspective it would appear that the business manager has limited scope for independent action. Power is exercised by the corporate group for the good of the owners and with the long-term interests of the business in mind. The corporate group act in four distinct ways, each aimed at actions that lead to gaining added value. The approaches include:

- monitoring and controlling the corporate process
- integrating the businesses to create synergies
- providing centralized functions and expertise
- influencing the scope and nature of the activities of the whole group.

This pressure, or conflict, between the corporate and the business managers, is a feature that determines attempts to control business decisions and performance. In order to exercise control, organizations break up the business development process into stages that can then be managed. The following review will help you to identify how you approach management and control of the business development process.

Reflect back to Reviews 5 and 6 (pages 112 and 117), where you identified the business idea that is driving the business direction and the key strategies that are being followed. Make a note, in the form of a statement, that captures how the business is unique, how it is structured to add value, and how it takes advantage of customer needs and the context in which it operates. Then answer the questions listed below.

_____

_____

_____

- What boundaries and controls did you place on the scope of your thinking about how the business idea is being implemented and supported?

_____

_____

_____

- What criteria did you use to determine whether the approach used to develop the business is proving effective?

_____

_____

_____

- To what extent are the original business idea, and subsequent strategic decisions, having a continuing influence on the development of the business?

_____

_____

_____

Reflect back to the Review 5 on page 112, where you identified areas in the business where there are mismatches between the business capabilities and the competitive environment. Make a note of these areas. Then answer the questions listed below.

■ What were the main sources of information that you used to form your views about these mismatches?

■ To what extent did you approach the analysis in a logical fashion and were your findings documented?

■ How valid would your identification of these mismatches be from the point of view of the dominant power group?

Reflect on the process used in your organization to debate and formulate business decisions. This could include decisions involving:

■ changes to the business direction

■ major long-term investment projects

■ changes to ownership of resources and forming of new partnerships and alliances

■ changes to organizational structures and processes.

Then answer the following questions.

■ To what extent is the information used to stimulate debate and is decision making in these areas well documented and made explicit?

■ Is the membership of the group that debates these issues sufficiently expert and informed to make effective decisions?

■ Are these debates and the resulting decisions well documented?

■ What measures are used to evaluate the effectiveness of these debates in determining a clear set of output decisions?

■ Is the process sufficiently linked and timely in terms of making decisions that directly benefit the business?

■ What measures are used to gauge the impact of these decisions on business performance?

_____

_____

_____

Having completed the above you are now in a position to conduct a detailed review of the key action areas within the business development process. Your ingrained approaches will determine the factors that you take into account when considering action and the measures you use to gauge the effectiveness of these actions. Use Fig. 9.2 to capture your findings.

Figure 9.2 **An audit of strategic actions and controls**

Area for action	Key contextual features that are taken into account	Measures used to gauge the success of the action	Confidence that the measure gives control
Identification of the business idea			
Determining the context in which the stages of the strategic management process are being played out			
Setting clear strategic direction and associated objectives			
Identifying the mix and detail of the generic strategies			
Identifying and making strategic decisions			
Selecting strategic options			
Implementing and controlling strategic decisions			

The traditional approach to controlling an activity is to set performance standards, establish measurement systems and use these to correct unsatisfactory performance. This approach to control is based on a two massive assumptions. The first is that the activity itself, if carried out as planned, will produce the desired output, and second that the measures being used to evaluate the results provide an accurate representation of the phenomena that we want to evaluate. In a nutshell, we assume that the speedometer reading allows us to gauge the level of risk involved in our driving maneuver and that a touch on the accelerator or the brake will result in a direct influence over this level of risk. We place great faith in this type of control system and have learned to take their operation for granted. But translating this belief to the complexity of the business world and expecting it to work is a bit more difficult.

Your reviews were centered around the process approach to evaluating the relationships between inputs and outputs. This approach is used to define and set up controls over the traditional stages in the business development process. For each stage there needs to be:

- a definition of the information that is required as an input
- a defined membership that has the appropriate expertise and commitment
- appointment of a leader or champion
- a clear set of controls
- agreement on a management style that facilitates the work of the members
- clear links to other stages in the business development process.

At first sight you may consider that this attention to detail far outweighs the benefits. You will have become used to a much more informal style of working when tackling business development. Familiarity between colleagues plus the political relationships and interests that are being pursued will have created either a cosy or confrontational atmosphere. If this is the case then the likelihood of any new or breakthrough thinking and action is unlikely to occur. In many organizations this uneasy peace becomes the norm. The process approach makes it possible to challenge ingrained thinking. So we need to take a look at how this process approach works.

The process approach

The business development process must be founded on a clear understanding of the business idea that is being used to drive the business. Also from a detailed knowledge of who the key players are that influence the decision making. In Review 13 you highlighted the significance of the dominant power group in formulating the business idea, the business direction and the key strategies. It is their business logic, how they make sense and form patterns from the complexity of the business situation that will influence these decisions. An indication of how these players and their thinking are contributing to the business development process can be seen by observing:

- the clarity and simplicity of any emerging policies
- the extent to which the outcomes of the process are understood and gain commitment from key players, both internal and external to the organization
- the perceived fit between the business idea and the business context
- the perceived fit of the strategies with the asset base and capabilities of the organization.

The extent to which these indications give you confidence that the process is working effectively will show you where changes to the process and controls have to be introduced.

Identifying the process used in the business to set direction and objectives will have highlighted the impact of the style used by the dominant power group and the experience levels of key executives. The company history and success in using control systems associated with objective setting will also be a major factor in determining how well this is done. Timeliness is a key issue here, in that where objectives and associated measures do not link closely to action taking, they are likely to be marginalized.

For example, analysis of the business context is often approached as though the environment is static. It is rarely viewed as a dynamic and changing scene where the various factors are interacting and influencing each other. The major influence on the quality of any contextual analysis will be the level of expertise, experience and knowledge of the key executives. The culture and history of the company will determine the extent to which this knowledge is shared and made explicit. But by establishing an effective process for reviewing the context you can improve the contribution this awareness makes to key business decisions. A measure of the quality of this process is in the clarity and shared understanding that colleagues have of the key contextual dynamics and also how closely linked the business strategies are to tangible measures of business performance in that context. Being able to discover and understand the links and relationships between implementation of a strategy and performance in a particular context is a key business development skill.

Your review of the decision-making process will have highlighted the need for clarity and effective measures of output. The interests of dominant stakeholders play a major part in how this process is conducted. Cynics would argue that it is in the interest of the power group to keep such processes away from outside influences. This may or may not be the case, but if it is then it cannot be in the best interests of the business. Exposure of the arguments and debates that develop from decision making, to a wide and informed audience, is essential to good business practice. We saw in an earlier review the importance of balancing stakeholder interests. This cannot be done by restricting the information required by these groups and constraining their ability to influence the outcomes. A clear process in this area ensures that executive energies are focused on highlighting and taking key decisions. Decisions in which all parties are involved and aware of the gains and potential losses to their particular interests. This will ensure that the power and interests of the business are focused on beating the competition and not on serving vested interests inside the organization.

The search for a winning business formula has been fuelled by the belief that generic strategies exist that can be applied in all contexts. Achieving the correct mix of cost leadership, differentiation and market focus strategies has underpinned the ambitions and plans of legions of business strategists. The review of how this process is carried out in your organization will have revealed that it is a lot less directive than is popularly believed. Matching generic strategies to the particular context is a key notion that drives business decision making. Here the measures used to gauge the success of the activity are a lot more familiar. By assuming that there are simple and clear links between these strategies and business performance, organizations establish output measures such as:

Matching generic strategies to the particular context is a key notion that drives business decision making

- financial ratios
- market share
- sales figures
- marketplace image
- customer loyalty
- competitor benchmark positioning.

Less obvious, but perhaps just as important, are measures such as:

- service response times
- stock and inventory levels
- staff turnover levels
- product design to commercialization time
- the degree and cost of innovation.

There are many other measures that organizations use as indications that they have the correct balance of the generic strategies. You need to constantly check that you have not fallen into the trap of assuming that an application of generic strategies has a direct impact on the outcomes and associated measures outlined above.

The final two areas in the review investigated the contextual factors and key measures that surround the selection of development options and their implementation. Here the power group have the greatest impact. They will be working within the constraints of the organizational climate and culture but are also influenced by the past history of the company. Balancing short-term and long-term ambitions and objectives will be a central focus of their efforts to make the right decisions and implement effective controls. Here the key role for the business manager is to be able to influence the agenda-setting process and the criteria against which business decisions are made.

SUMMARY

You have now completed the two areas of review that underpin the skill of taking action in context. We saw the importance of obtaining a clear view of the overall purpose of the organization. We also saw that opinions varied over whose interests the organization should be serving. The primacy of the shareholder competing with views that argued for the total stakeholders' interests to be the ones that the organization must address. It is this process of attempting to gauge and balance the interests of these groups that creates the organizational dynamics. Without these pressures the business will quickly find itself out of tune with its environment. The traditional pressure was seen to come from the external funding groups and those who provide the credibility that the firm relies on for survival in the financial marketplace. This raised the issue of ownership and the importance attached to the executive role of providing shareholders with a clear view as to the risks and returns attached to investment in the business. Here we saw a conflict arising in that some executive decisions may be focused on the longer-term performance, whereas the investors may judge that short-term profits should be taken. How long investors are willing to wait for a profitable realization from their investment is a judgement that many boards have got wrong.

The need to balance internal interests was also highlighted. The notion that all the internal groups are focused on the same goals is idealistic and probably undesirable. The tension that differing interests create is the dynamic that enables the organization to remain competitive. The danger is in failing to strike a balance between the internal and external interests groups. Here we saw the benefits of an organization subscribing to a higher order set of social values. A business that accepts and fulfils this wider social responsibility is seen as being more likely to survive and prosper in the long run. This can be encouraged by helping colleagues to express their perspectives on:

- the prime purpose of the business
- how they attribute value to the interests of the various stakeholder groups
- their stance regarding the social responsibility of the business.

These are the beliefs and values that will underpin their decision making and commitment to action.

We also explored the question of how to apply controls and evaluate outcomes of the stages in the business development process. We saw that the stages do not necessarily follow in a sequential order and that no organization is likely to be starting with a blank sheet. By adopting a process approach we were able to see how key stages are characterized by informal approaches. Familiarity, tacit agreements about personal boundaries, and conventional wisdom, were all seen as mitigating against any radical changes being proposed. The benefits of familiarity and shared understanding are of enormous value to a business but they can also result in a lack of flexibility and responsiveness.

The purpose of the business development process is to evolve winning strategies. We have seen that determining a new strategy or recommending changes to the existing ones is not difficult. But to be effective a strategy has to be recognized and accepted by the power group and the operational managers. The following guidelines can be used to check whether your proposals are likely to meet those requirements. Namely that the strategy:

- must be coherent and follow from a proposition and analysis that can be readily communicated and understood. It must be consistent with the purpose of the organization and be seen as meeting the requirements of the key stakeholders
- should be based on addressing the key issues in the environment that have a longer-term influence on the business and should not be simply tactical
- should be easily linked to the vision and strategic intent of the organization and likely to be supported over sufficient time to realize tangible results in spite of setbacks and barriers
- needs to be: clear, supportable and robust. In summary, the strategy must follow from and help to develop the business idea that is driving the business
- must be timed in such a way that other events, which are likely to impact on the success of the strategy, have been anticipated and can be treated as a managed risk. Short-term pressures on the business must not be such that they place the success of the launch and development of the strategy at risk
- must be capable of making a clear and tangible contribution to the sustainable competitive advantage of the business. It must have obvious advantages over competing strategies in the eyes of the executives and managers who will be involved in its launch and development
- must be congruent with the capabilities over which the organization has control. This includes: the management expertise, the required knowledge base, the human and physical resources, financial resources and any outside networks and alliances.

▶

■ must be capable of attracting and gaining the support of interest groups both inside and outside the organization.

Quite a tall order, and not many proposals for change would stand up to these requirements. But success in your personal and work life will depend on selling your ideas and gaining support for new business strategies. To do this effectively you need to acquire the final two generic skills: the ability to adapt, and to use intuition.

Part **3** c

Developing your strategic
sense and imagination

10

Learning how to adapt

Harnessing your creativity

Adapting to new situations and ideas is not easy as it runs counter to our basic approach to making sense of complexity. In order to deal with the uncertainties and ambiguities that surround business development we seek ways to frame and stabilize our perceptions. The steps are well ingrained in the management psyche:

- establish and measure the gap between desired and actual business performance
- identify the factors in the business context and their causal relationships as a means of detecting patterns and trends
- use familiar explanatory frameworks and knowledge to generate confidence in the patterns that have been detected
- rely on rationalization and logical argument to remove uncertainties and clarify ambiguities
- rely on cynicism, the use of premise statements and personal power to rebuff any serious challenges to the rationalizations and logic
- rely on the strength of the group and the organizational culture to validate your framework and arguments.

This process is found in all organizations. It works and is well understood. So why would I ask you to think of challenging conventional wisdom? Quite simply because it does not help either you or the organization to learn how to adapt. It simply reinforces accepted learning and the existing organizational paradigm.

Dealing with the complexities involved in developing a business presents us with a paradox. On the one hand we can see the value of resolving the uncertainties by constructing explanatory frameworks as a basis for rational decision making. But on the other hand we know that development comes from challenging existing knowledge and from embracing complexity. To deal with this paradox by adopting defensive positions would be foolhardy. At one extreme it would result in the organization exhibiting an obdurate and oppressive form of behavior and at the other, behavior that was unstable and egocentric. You may have experienced both of these extremes. But the way forward lies in using the ideas in this paradox as a source of inspiration from which to develop the ability to adapt. It provides an opportunity to harness both our own creativity and that of our colleagues to find new ways of thinking and challenging ingrained approaches. To do this we need to understand and harness our own and our colleagues' creative abilities.

Dealing with the complexities involved in developing a business presents us with a paradox

Creativity can be developed

At first sight creativity appears to be a gift and it seems that some of us are naturally more creative than others. But with more careful consideration we discover that the ability to generate novel ways of interpreting and framing a situation depends on our perception of the complexity of the issues involved. It also has a lot to do with our determination to make sense of the situation. For example, if we perceive that the issues are predictable and clear, then a formal or structured approach will confirm our existing beliefs and past experiences. This applies to the majority of operational decisions that we face. Proposals to use a more creative or unstructured approach are rejected as introducing unnecessary complications and slowing down decision making and action taking. But where the perception is that the issue is complex and ambiguous then adopting a structured approach simply submerges the ambiguity. With a structured approach logic and rhetoric soon dominate the process. Complex issues justify a more creative or unstructured approach. Here the status quo is challenged and unique perceptions and frameworks are valued and developed.

Complex issues justify a more creative or unstructured approach

There are obviously hundreds of problems and issues that arise as a business develops and grows. The key to using creativity to adapt and learn from these events is in separating those that call for a rational approach from those that will benefit from new thinking. How you make this interpretation will depend on your ability to use creative techniques, the organizational culture and your cognitive style. You should check back to Review 4, where you identified your cognitive style, and Review 10, where you identified the dominant organizational culture. Then complete the following review. This will help you to evaluate how adaptable you are when faced with complexity and events that demand original thinking. It will also indicate how and where you need to improve your ability to harness the power of creativity and to adapt.

REVIEW 16

Think of an incident or event in your career when you came into contact with someone whom you consider to be creative. Would you consider that this person was:

- inherently gifted?

- able to remove mental constraints?

- just in the right place at the right time?

- skilled at using novel associations?

- a lifelong practitioner in the business area and able to notice and capture anomalies?

Which of these characteristics match your own ability to demonstrate creativity?

_____

_____

_____

Which of the following features or characteristics do you feel that you possess and are likely to exhibit when faced with a complex business issue or when engaged in strategic thinking?

- a high tolerance for ambiguity

- an ability to excel at finding problems, e.g. winnowing out ideas

- an ability to conduct mental gymnastics, e.g. often thinking in metaphors

- a willingness to take risks, e.g. constantly seeking excitement

- an ability to accept failure, e.g. not expecting every idea to be a breakthrough

- an ability to be objective and seek out criticism.

_____

_____

_____

Think about a recent situation where you were working with others to tackle a work issue. Then answer the following questions:

- How important was it to generate a completely new approach to framing and representing the issue?
- Was your approach adaptive or innovative? (See Fig. 6.6 for definitions.)
- On reflection, was your approach appropriate in the circumstances?
- How aware were you of the mix of cognitive styles among your colleagues?
- Faced with a similar situation would you change your approach to framing the issue?

_____

_____

_____

REVIEW 17

In this review, assume that you are leading the business development team in a major transport and logistics company. You have received a report on the business from a leading consultancy firm, shown below. You are planning to use it at a meeting that will include the heads of the various operational functions, the business managers and the chief executive. Your intention is to challenge the way that you and your colleagues currently view the business idea and the business direction. The consultant's report is given below.

Consultant's report

The success of the firm has, in the past, been based on an ability to provide warehousing and distribution services to blue-chip retailers on a national basis. The firm has, over the years, been able to attract high margins through a mixture of skilful contract negotiation and control and expertise in the design and management of dedicated warehousing facilities. The business planning and control processes and procedures are very well defined and it would be difficult to find a firm, in the industry, that could improve on the methods of financial control being used. Your major blue-chip clients are locked into five- to ten-year contracts, but many of these are due to expire within 12 months. The marketplace has changed and the firm is now facing clients who want lower prices and more flexible contracts. The competition is very active in this area and is willing to negotiate new contract conditions with any interested client. The competitors are showing all the *entrepreneurial skills that your firm apparently had 20 years ago when it was formed. Our observation is that the business managers and operational staff in your firm are wedded to the old methods of contracting and working. They will be very reluctant or even unable to change their mental images of how the business should be driven and their ways of working. It could be that the future of the firm depends on being able to introduce some radical changes to business practices, while recognizing that there is a large asset base and a well-trained workforce that is currently keeping you as Number 1 in the industry.*

The following guide and questions will help you to prepare for your meeting. The first step is to consider how to describe the way that the group currently views the business. This will include outlining the business idea, the features of the business context, links between elements in the business context and the dependencies the business has on outside agencies. You need to present this interpretive framework at a level of detail appropriate for this audience.

The second step is to propose a framework to challenge the recipe or formula being used by your colleagues. Your intention is to reach agreement on the future direction to be taken by the business.

Step 1

Describe the business idea and business logic that is currently being used by senior management. You may find that it easier to do this by using a mixture of diagrams and text.

Step 2

Describe the changes to the business idea and business logic that you would present to the senior management.

What are the key features of your planned approach to this meeting?

_____

_____

_____

Which aspects or activities in Steps 1 and 2 presented you with the greatest difficulties?

_____

_____

_____

On reflection, do you consider that your approach demonstrated a sufficiently high level of creative thinking? If not, then what constraints did you experience?

_____

_____

_____

Your reflections about creative people you have worked with will have confirmed that creativity has more to do with perspiration than inspiration. Einstein, Bill Gates and whoever else you consider to be creative did not just stumble across a winning formula. There is some truth in the saying about "Being in the right place at the right time," but that is only a part of the story. It is possible to improve the ability to be creative by adopting a positive approach to problem solving, seeing setbacks as an opportunity for learning rather than as an indication of a lack of creativity. The ability to accept the ambiguity in a situation also suggests that an attitude of mind that errs on the playful side is an asset when facing complex situations. But the main characteristic that you need is persistence and a passion that will sustain you even when faced with major setbacks and obstacles.

Cognitive style

Your cognitive style has a major bearing on how you set about making sense of complex issues. If your style is predominantly adaptive then you will prefer to collect the facts, be clear over what has to be achieved, and ascertain the boundaries and constraints before considering ways forward. But if your style is highly innovative then free thinking is likely to characterize your approach. Both of these styles are creative, but the approaches used are quite different. The key is to be aware of your style but more importantly, to recognize when it clashes with those of your colleagues. A highly innovative style can be easily interpreted as impractical whereas the highly adaptive style is often seen as being constrained and unimaginative.

In asking you to tackle the transport company case study, my intention was to test out your approach to helping others adapt. Enabling you to see how effective you are in using creativity as part of the adaptation process. But first we need to look at the case itself.

Case analysis

The consultant's report sounds very convincing. On the one hand, it is congratulating the firm on being very strong on traditional management planning and control and confirming that this is the factor that has made the firm the market leader. On the other hand, it warns that this very strength may become a weakness as the market has changed and the competition have responded by being adaptive to the new demands of the marketplace and their clients. The case also presents a classic example of where the business idea being used to drive a business is no longer in tune with the context for which it was originally designed. The original business was centered around skilled contract negotiation, warehousing expertise, and employing tight controls to keep costs low and monitor service performance levels. The marketing thrust had been targeted at gaining loyalty from a select group of large blue-chip clients. The business idea and the supporting strategies and structures provided a clear set of signals to the operational staff and the business managers as to what was important. This allowed them to concentrate on incremental improvements aimed at optimizing the use of resources and improving the margins. The success of all of this effort depended on the blue-chip clients being able to live with the costs while continuing to want to outsource their logistics activities and seeing the value in having long-term contract relationships with one supplier.

Having captured the logic that your colleagues were using to make sense of the business you were then faced with the problem of how to take this thinking forward. How radical or boundary breaking were you able to be? Or did you focus on maintaining the status quo? One approach could have been to suggest that a new business division had to be set up. A business focused on entrepreneurial activities that would replicate the moves of the competition and seek to develop breakthrough strategies for doing business with large clients. The idea being that the main organization had to be kept intact, with organizational renewal concentrated in the new business division. An alternative, and less radical, approach would have been to spur the organization towards achieving greater cost cutting while attempting to find new ways of securing the loyalty of existing blue-chip clients, denigrating any moves by competitors that professed to offer a better service. A longer-term strategic approach would be to argue that the organizational culture had to be changed but that the original business idea and strategies would remain intact.

The significance of anomalies

The fundamental problem facing the company was to determine whether the consultants had identified a minor anomaly or whether the report signalled the need to breakout of the current mental paradigm. For many companies this area of decision making is badly managed. Management teams become wedded to recipes for operating and developing a business. Adapting their thinking to take account of changes in the business context is a skill that few possess. An effective way in which this adaptability can be improved is to recognize that anomalies occur and have a management process in place that enables the executive to address them. Figure 10.1 indicates the way in which anomalies can be identified and integrated into the business development process.

We have accepted that in order for a firm to sustain a position of competitive advantage it must have a clear focus on meeting targeted objectives. Yet at the same time it must allow business managers to explore and find the way

Figure 10.1 Making use of anomalies

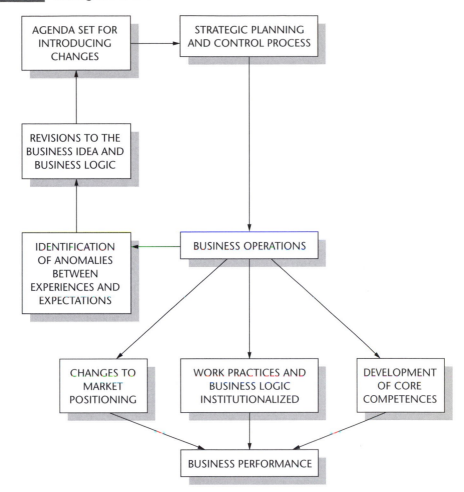

forward. This more risk-laden exploration takes as inputs the anomalies that arise from everyday actions that occur in running the business. The reasoning behind this belief is that the conventional approach to business development relies on introducing incremental changes. This generates anomalies, or signals, that do not fit easily into the models held by the managers, and unless the discontinuities are so large that attention has to be paid to them, then they are reduced to an informal or tacit level in the organizational conversation. As a manager you need to recognize these signals as inputs to the formal business development process. Their significance must be highlighted if these new ideas are to be accepted into the business. Within this approach you can see that adaptability can benefit from harnessing your ability to be creative and think in new ways, but that this needs to be linked to establishing and accelerating the way in which you learn.

Accelerating your learning

There are two areas where learning becomes crucial to our ability to adapt in business and social settings. The first area is where we learn the technical skills associated with modelling a business situation as a simple quantifiable game. A style of learning that results in decision rules and industry recipes becoming institutionalized. The focus is on learning to adapt the information and knowledge that we have to familiar frameworks and models. It is essential that we are able to do this as it enables us to make decisions and rationalize over events that do not fit the models and the assumptions on which they are built. This is a vital form of learning as it allows us to focus on the job in hand as opposed to constantly being distracted by anomalies. We quickly develop defensive routines and an organizational language that reinforce this type of learning. The downside is that it can create both personal and organizational myopia. We become less open to being able to learn from our mistakes.

The second area of learning arises from using these adaptive frameworks and models to manage our strategic behavior. While doing this we are confronted with having to deal with mismatches between our own learned frameworks and those of our colleagues. Most of this second level, or meta learning, is done at a tacit level. At this tacit level we learn to close the gaps between how we make sense of the complexities of situations and how others make sense of them. Our learning becomes quickly ingrained and is rarely raised to an explicit level. We adapt at a tacit level but rarely translate that adaptation into behavior. What we have to learn to do is to use these perceived mismatches to accelerate our learning. The learning has to become generative and take our thinking and action beyond the incremental approaches that we use for adaption. We have to learn how to generate new ways of interpreting the application of our adaptive models and how to feed back that learning to influence our actions. By doing this we will gain the benefits from adaptive learning and from breakthrough or generative learning. We now need to tackle a review of your current approach to learning and then investigate ways in which that learning can be accelerated.

REVIEW 18

Read the two cases given below and tackle the questions that follow.

Case 1

A software company received a large number of complaints about a new release of an operating system that they had developed for a client server application. The complaints concerned the high number of software "bugs" that were being experienced with the new release. The level was perceived, by customers, as being far greater than had ever been experienced with earlier versions. The response made by the Director of Operations was to put more people on the "help desk" and to pressurize the design engineers to improve the rate at which they investigated and resolved the "bugs."

Accepting the point that an operational response had to be made, how would you represent this response in terms of an adaptation to the initial interpretive framework being used by the operations manager? Your representation should be in the form of a flow diagram involving the activities and links between the software design activity and the customer application. Show how the flow diagram was changed to accommodate the customer complaint.

If you were asked to interpret the above situation from a longer-term business perspective, what actions would have to be considered? Furthermore, how could these changes be reflected into the adaptive model being used by the Operations Director?

_____

_____

_____

Case 2

Co-operation between the four divisions of a major company had deteriorated to the point where major improvements in the manufacturing processes in one division were not being shared across the company. The result was a failure to meet an increase in worldwide demand for a key product. The response from the Executive Director for Manufacturing was to introduce a communications program across the divisions in order to accelerate the transfer of manufacturing knowledge.

Assume that you are a management consultant and have been brought in to help accelerate and improve the business development capability of the senior executives. What questions would you put to the Executive Director of Manufacturing in order to:

■ expose the interpretive framework being used to drive the operational thinking in the manufacturing function

■ draw out and make explicit the thinking that resulted in the decision to set up the communications program as an adaptive response

■ help explore additional areas in the interpretive framework that had contributed to the failure of the company to meet worldwide demand for the product

■ encourage the use of this failure as a stimulus to engage in some generative learning, stretching the boundaries of the adaptive model by confronting the strategic issues that this failure to perform has highlighted.

_____

_____

_____

Reflect back to a major business success and a major failure that you have been involved in or have observed closely over the past two years. What did you learn about your ability to adapt your thinking as to what contributes to the success of a business?

_____

_____

_____

Reflect back to a major surprise or something that stands out as having caused you to change your understanding of what makes a business successful. Use Fig. 10.2 to indicate the event and whether you see this as an example of adaptive or generative learning and the level at which the learning is held.

Figure 10.2 **Adaptive and generative learning**

Timescale	Event	Adaptive	Generative	At a tacit or explicit level?
0–6 months				
6–12 months				
12–18 months				
18–24 months				

COMMENTARY

You will have found that generating simple but robust frameworks that capture complex business operations is not easy. But the point that this review has brought out is that short-term responses to business events always result in adaptation of a simple interpretation. In the case of the software company the response was based on improving the response capability of the operation. Throwing more resources at the points in the system where capacity was seen to be blocking the ability to respond. This is a classic example of adaptive learning. One where a highly experienced operations manager uses an interpretive framework that lends itself to easy identification of the problem. This type of framing, decision making, and action taking is the ultimate aim of many organizations. It would take a major or near cataclysmic event to occur before the interpretive framework would be seriously questioned. But when we take a more strategic perspective of this situation we might question:

- the performance measures being used to gauge the effectiveness of the design process
- the effectiveness of the quality assurance process
- the need for a fundamental review of the applications and support services being provided to customers.

In the second case you were asked to formulate questions that would expose the way in which the manufacturing executive used an adaptive approach. This is not an easy task and you will have noticed how questioning someone about the framework that they are using to drive their thinking can be potentially threatening. You probably wanted to ask questions that probed:

- the variations in capability and expertise across the divisions
- the thinking behind the policy decision to disperse manufacturing across the divisions
- the effectiveness of the divisional managers
- the effectiveness and relevance of any quality assurance programs
- the relationships and interface between design, manufacturing, stocking policies and demand scheduling.

The point being made in both of these cases is that accelerating individual and organizational learning is best done around real issues. Your learning stems from taking action. Where the desired level of performance is being met then the frameworks and perspectives being used are rarely questioned. Any learning will be adaptive and demands to change these frameworks will be interpreted as exhortations unless supported by hard evidence of the benefits that will transpire. This is known as "single loop learning" where the interpretive mental models are honed to perfection. Generative learning requires that you challenge the values that have been used to build and maintain these models. Our values and beliefs about the business are often established from events that occurred in a particular set of circumstances. It is likely that as the circumstances change we fail to update these values and beliefs. The frameworks that we have so painstakingly honed will, at best, give us a false interpretation of events and, at worst, lead us into making disastrous personal and business decisions. Your review of a major success and a major failure will have made this point clear.

Confront basic assumptions

We have seen that in order to accelerate generative learning you have to practice unearthing and confronting your basic assumptions as well as those held by your colleagues. Areas where this questioning can be applied include:

- the values and motives that underpin your longer term business and personal goals

- the reasoning used to establish boundaries to business and personal development concerns

- the relevance and value of the performance measures used in the business and personal development

- the use being made of the tensions that result from mismatches between your expectations and performance concerning business and personal agendas.

Use metaphor and dialogue

Contemporary advice on how best to unearth the mental models that managers use to drive their thinking varies enormously. But a good way to start involves building on your previous experiences of using metaphor and dialogue. From this it is possible to establish a simple process that will accelerate your abilities as an adaptive and as a generative learner. There are four steps in this process.

1. Create an environment in which you can engage in a dialogue with colleagues over key work issues. The dialogue should be aimed at taking you far beyond the normal debates that are held. Bring in outsiders who can provide new and deeper insights into how tacit knowledge is being used to drive the thinking.

2. Turn the tacit knowledge that emerges into explicit concepts by the use of shared metaphors, analogies, concepts and models. The use of metaphor and analogy is a key to the success of this step. It is important that you prioritize the areas that you wish to test out.

3. Turn the concepts into knowledge that can be shared and referenced to a wider set of events and settings, opening up the boundaries to your thinking and perception.

4. Capture this new knowledge and integrate it into your formal processes for establishing priorities and making decisions. Set up measures by which the pay-off from using this new knowledge can be evaluated.

SUMMARY

You have now completed the reviews that underpin the skill of mastering the adaptation process. This is a skill that will underpin development of an overarching strategy between your personal and corporate agendas. We saw that creativity has a major part to play in adaptive learning and how successful businesses and individuals thrive on such learning. Capturing and making explicit the learning that has taken place relies on being able to confront established and proven mental models. It is also important to be able to judge when a framebreaking approach is required. That it is no good waiting until we become moribund before deciding that the tramline thinking has to be challenged. Framebreaking is not simply the domain of the original thinker. Most businesses and individuals thrive on implementing fairly obvious ideas, whereas developing new ways of thinking is possible if we simply tap into our inherent creativity.

The reviews will have confirmed that the best source of personal learning is the business itself. Taking action around real issues and grappling with the mental models and perspectives held by powerful colleagues provides the ideal setting. This does mean confronting deeply held values and beliefs. But confrontation based on a determination driven from a clarity of purpose and integrity will result in benefits to yourself and the business. As we move to our sixth and final skill, using intuition, I will show you how the link between personal and corporate agendas can be completed.

Intuition, the ultimate skill

Developing vision

You are now being invited to tackle the most abstract and elusive of the generic skills, that of using your intuition. Intuition becomes your sixth sense. A sense that relies heavily on your talents as a visionary and the ability to let your imagination drive your thinking. But first we need to look a bit closer at what is required of a visionary and how this can be linked to developing personal and work agendas.

The role of a visionary

In earlier reviews we saw that the role of the leader is often synonymous with that of the visionary. Followers expect the leader to set the scene and be able to envisage their collective futures. In a corporate world the senior team strive to come to a collective vision of the future that they are then expected to articulate to their colleagues and followers. We might argue about the process by which the vision is established but rarely question the original inspiration or source from which it sprang. The traditional view is that a vision derives from a combination of strong leadership, an ability to imagine the future and a clear view of how events will conspire to create that future. I believe that this view about the true leader who will envision and safeguard our future, is deeply rooted in our psyche.

There are two powerful notions driving our concern to capture a vision for our careers and the business we are charged with developing. First, that events will follow a conventional life cycle and second, that competition in a free market will eventually erode away any competitive advantage that we may have. We respond to these drives by working harder to sustain any competitive advantage by making incremental improvements. These efforts are encapsulated in what becomes our strategic vision for our career and for the business. But contemporary thinking suggests that we must develop a vision that encompasses not only our current activities but also those we will meet in the future. This notion of renewal and rebirth is very powerful and is the area in which your skills as a visionary need to be honed. A review of your current approach to developing the business will help you assess your skills in this area.

REVIEW 19

Reflect back to the Review 6 on page 117, where you considered the development of your current business. Then answer the following questions:

- Can the core businesses generate sufficient earnings to support investment in a growth strategy and which areas should you concentrate on?

- Assume that the business continues to pursue an incremental growth strategy. Over what time horizon is it likely to be able to support the ambitions of the dominant stakeholders?

- At what point in the future do you envisage that a more radical innovation strategy will be required if the business is to continue to grow?

- Which of the following six areas would you search in to find opportunities that go beyond the notion of growing the business through incremental improvements:

  – existing customers, products and services?

  – new customer groups, products and services?

  – new patterns of operation and methods of delivering products and services?

  – new regions and countries?

  – by changing the industry boundaries, structures and ways of trading?

  – by moving into new industry sectors and crossing value chain boundaries?

Reflect on ideas that you have had over the past year about how to take the organization beyond the current business thinking. Then answer the following questions:

- What new business ideas have you considered?

- How long is it since you first thought of these ideas and what response have you had from colleagues?

- Do colleagues see your ideas as being radical and ground-breaking?

_____

_____

_____

Think of three suggestions for making changes to the dominant business idea that you, or one of your colleagues, have raised over the last 12 months. Rate these ideas in terms of their compatibility with the current capability of the firm and their attractiveness in terms of the level of enthusiasm and passion behind the idea. Use Fig. 11.1 to record your findings.

Figure 11.1 Potential changes to the business idea

	Passionate	Excited	Enthusiastic	Interested	Casual
Incompatible					
Poor fit					
Fits					
Good fit					
Perfect fit					

If you were asked to set up a new venture team within your organization, what specific problems would you expect to encounter in terms of:

- reaching a clear definition of the business idea to be pursued by the new venture team?

- maintaining the impetus required to carry the venture through to commercialization?

- balancing the strategic direction involved in the new venture with that being followed by the business?

- obtaining support from the functional and operational groups in the organization?

The review will have highlighted a key paradox that underpins thinking about personal and business growth. Experience tells us that success comes from developing a perfect fit between our capabilities and market opportunities and that we can achieve this fit by adopting a process of incremental improvement. While at the same time we must be open to recognizing and creating new opportunities that, if seized, will establish our link to continuing success. To do this we have to adopt a process of radical innovation. Recognizing this paradox and finding a way of managing it differentiates those who will succeed from the rest. Being able to communicate a vision that is relevant and takes account of the here and now while you simultaneously embrace the creation of a new vision is the skill that you need to develop. The mistake that many people make is to fail to see this need to hold simultaneously overlapping as well as discontinuous visions.

> We must be open to recognizing and creating new opportunities that, if seized, will establish our link to continuing success

As our personal and business situations develop then our vision helps us to adapt and incorporate changes in order to gain competitive advantage. It is vital that we maintain a clear approach to growth and evolve a set of managed strategies using the vision to maintain long-term continuity around these efforts. But at some point we have to begin searching for opportunities to create a more stretching vision. A vision that may well be at odds with the one that is currently providing satisfaction.

Searching for growth opportunities

In the review I highlighted six areas in which new opportunities for business growth could be explored. While doing this your thinking will have been driven by a mind-set based on your understanding the current business thinking and vision. For example, when looking for growth opportunities among existing customers, products and services, or for new patterns of operation, the tendency is to seek incremental improvements to what already exists. But new thinking also stems from such searches. An example here would be with the cellular phone companies who have sought growth in consumer as opposed to corporate markets. This has resulted in them promoting the cellular phone as a fashion accessory. Breaking out of a mind-set dominated by technological applications has enabled some of these companies to move rapidly into alliances that have moved their business vision to one of seeing themselves in the multi-media business. There are many examples of this happening in banking, retailing and the financial services industries.

A more challenging but less familiar area in which to search for growth is to move your thinking outside the current industry boundaries. This goes far beyond strategies involving vertical and horizontal integration. For example, some businesses have managed to apply their existing competences in ways that enable them to link into value chains in other industries. Others have transferred technology and their learning and developments in operational practice from one industry into another and in so doing, completely changing the rules of the game. A classic example of this is how e-business technology is now being used to break the rules of the strategy game in many industries. Software development capabilities and expertise in telecommunications is being applied to revolutionalize traditional and well-established trading and business activities.

Being a visionary

You now have a good insight into how important it is to maintain a clear vision that can be used to drive business and personal development while looking for the break-out vision. The contemporary view is that successful companies have learned how to develop and manage not two, but three overlapping visions. The first is the one that drives the current core business and gives overall focus and direction. The second or emerging vision begins to incorporate the entrepreneurial thinking and the opportunities that are being pursued to grow the current business. Eventually this emerging vision will replace the original one. The third goes beyond the pipedreams generated at company away-days. Specific options for new business ideas have to be declared and followed up. Alliances with potential partners for new idea investigation, networking with groups that are not involved in your industry and commitment of funds to sponsor research are all obvious ways in which this third vision can be developed.

In most businesses the change from the first to the second vision is imperceptible and is closely linked to the strategic investment decision process and corporate venturing. With corporate venturing the company often sets up a new division that maintains close links with the dominant corporate strategies. The challenge to managing these new ventures is that of ensuring that the current business mind-sets do not overly inhibit the changes to the core business that their growth requires. The dilemma that this presents is how to manage the trade-offs that have to be made between investment required in developing key products in the new venture with the support required to grow and develop the existing business. Although this may seem like a statement of the obvious, it is an area of management decision making that constrains the growth and ultimate survival of many companies. Here conventional wisdom tells us that the success of these new ventures depends on:

- enthusiastic corporate championing and support
- a belief that only by this process will a new vision be created and the future business survival be assured
- a continuing dialogue between those involved in the core business and those in the new venture is maintained.

You have now seen what is required of you as a visionary in the business. The traditional belief that successful individuals are those that pursue an unequivocal vision has to be challenged. This becomes apparent when we consider the process that is involved in establishing a vision. First, the ideas surrounding the opportunities for the future have to be generated. This requires a deep understanding of a particular setting and the major forces as well as opportunities that are likely to exist. Such an understanding can only be found in the minds of those who have had a great deal of exposure to that particular setting. We also know from our previous experiences that a vision only becomes useful when those who are going to be involved can recognize it and give it their commitment. The very process of presentation and dialogue creates a two-way process from which the vision will emerge. The vision has to be tempered on this hotbed of dialogue and debate, as without this process it will not have any true impact on the direction of the business. Within, and perhaps underpinning most of the activities involved in developing a vision, is the use of imagination.

Using your imagination

Not many managers would admit that they relied on imagination when trying to make sense of an anomaly or deal with a business decision. I suspect that you, like others, have also been chided by colleagues for having a rich imagination and been left with a feeling of uncertainty as to whether this was a compliment or a criticism. In organizations we find a continuing love-hate relationship between those who profess to be deeply logical and predictable and those who appear to make use of their imagination to challenge the conventional wisdom. These styles are accentuated and become much more obvious when tackling unstructured problems.

In everyday life we are quite happy to rely on our intuition in a number of ways. We use it to:

- detect when an event or occurrence needs to be framed as a problem
- create patterns that help make sense of the mass of data that we receive
- gauge the significance and put a value on the outcomes of the analytical approaches taken to understanding a situation.

Looked at in this way we can see a close link between the more rational approaches to making sense of a situation and the use of intuition. It is seeing this link that opens the door to us making much more use of our intuition. But the process can be accelerated if we learn to make use of our imagination.

Theorists tell us that the concepts that we rely on to make sense of business are, in fact, mental images of things, acts and relationships. Further, that how we string these concepts together and apply them is a measure of our ability to apply our imagination. It is not feasible for us to force ourselves to imagine solutions to problems or to come up with a new business vision. Yet I would suggest that this is what most of us do automatically when faced with complexity. Given a complex set of data and an interesting proposition to tackle we really want to make sense of the whole thing quickly. We are driven by a desire to resolve the complexity, to see the hidden links and to be able to tell our colleagues that we have seen the patterns and the solutions. In doing this we are forcing ourselves to imagine the solution. But experience tells us that this rarely happens, so the tendency is to constrain this desire to take that imaginative leap. But what we can do is to engage with others in a process of communication and sharing of mental maps, metaphors and analogies so that we can feel our way forward. Imagining is a key skill used in that process. Completing the next review will show you how you use your imagination in developing the business.

REVIEW 20

Earlier reviews gave you a good feel for the context in which your business is operating. I would like you to produce a list showing which of the areas in that environment you are most uncertain about in terms of possible changes and their impact on the business over the next three years. An area of uncertainty is where you are worried that the changes in that area, could cause a downturn in business or operational performance. Against each area reflect on the source of your uncertainty. These sources may include:

- personal exposure and business experience
- research findings, reading reports and industry articles
- conversations and debates with colleagues
- intuition and gut feel
- others sources.

Use Fig. 11.2 overleaf to capture your thinking.

Figure 11.2 Areas of uncertainty

	Experience	Research	Colleagues	Intuition	Other sources
Area 1					
Area 2					
Area 3					
Area 4					
Area 5					

Select from the list one area where your uncertainty was based on research findings and one where it was based on intuition. For each area define the items or constituent features that make up that area. You need to be confident that the level of precision in your definitions match those required in a consultancy report.

Uncertainty based on research findings

_____

_____

_____

Uncertainty based on intuition

_____

_____

_____

Reflect on how the quality of your definitions varied. What has this exercise done to your confidence that you can now anticipate the impact on the business of these two areas?

_____

Reflect on how you tackled the above review. Using the following questions as a guide for this reflection. Remember to ask yourself "Why was this so?" after each question.

- What level of enthusiasm did you experience when tackling this task?

- Did you find it hard or easy to produce a description of the five areas and the information required to detail the features in the two areas that you selected? What was the source of any difficulty?

- Did your confidence in the level of detail that you were using vary during the exercise?

_____

_____

_____

The above exercise will have given you a much clearer insight into the future environments in which your business may find itself competing. Now use the following questions to probe the extent to which your imagination is guiding your thinking about how the business should react to the findings from your review.

- Will the current business idea be able to prosper in the future business context that you have envisaged? If not, in what way does the business idea need to be changed?

- Are the key strategies being used to develop the business appropriate in the future business context that you have envisaged? If not, what changes need to be made to these strategies?

- What level of credence and support would you give to the view that the best way to handle the future is to manipulate the features in the business context so that they fit the current business idea and key strategies, i.e. that the focus should be on creating a sympathetic context for the developing business?

_____

_____

_____

COMMENTARY

This review presented you with some exciting challenges. The construction of possible future scenarios for your business brings into play your experience, knowledge, motivation, creativity and imagination, all of which will have been heavily influenced by the context in which your business exists. For example, the patterns that can be seen in the business contexts of retail, pharmaceutical and financial services companies vary enormously. But although the contexts vary, our ability to use our imagination to determine possible futures is a skill that can be developed. You may have been surprised to find that you place such a high level of confidence in your intuitive ability to sense uncertainty in a situation, or alternatively that you rely totally on substantive data. This confirms that we are prepared to make casual interpretations of areas in the business that we judge as being trivial and unimportant, but that as the areas start to infringe on our deeply held beliefs and personal motivations then we either rely totally on intuition to defend our understanding or on hard facts. My contention is that we use intuition to defend areas that are close to our feelings and major drives. Hence if we are going to change or question these feelings then the only way we can do this is by exercising our imaginations. It is only when we decide to give up our neat and proven prescriptions for dealing with problems and uncertainty that we begin to create a new understanding.

Develop your intuition

Using imagination to deal with uncertainty smacks to some as just guessing. But when we are confronted with complex business situations, the need to out-think the competition and to satisfy a range of stakeholders, we are not going to be able to rely on logic or simple rules. Our thoughts and actions are going to rely on the use of judgement, intuition and using our imagination to see patterns among the complexity. We need to find ways of combining feelings and facts to see new possibilities in a business situation. This skill may be easier to develop where you are exposed to situations that do not lend themselves to actions and solutions that can be evaluated easily. Constantly working at operational level problems and with well-defined procedures and processes limits your opportunities to practice this skill.

We need to find ways of combining feelings and facts to see new possibilities in a business situation

Business development is the area that is most likely to put demands on your intuitive skills. In these situations you will find yourself faced with:

- a high level of uncertainty
- information that is ambiguous at best
- a lack of previous exposure
- rhetorical and persuasive arguments from colleagues
- pressure to clarify issues and make decisions
- feelings that you associate with being in a high-risk situation
- a feeling that you are being forced into the position of having to rely on your judgement.

Experience tells us that we find it easy to rely on intuition when the feeling that we are right is very strong. This feeling is easily communicated to colleagues and our enthusiasm drives through many of the obstacles and uncertainties that we experience. Based on this evidence we need to learn to value the strength of these intuitive skills, to learn to let imagination and emotions take control of our thinking so that the intuitive senses can surface. For some people this state is best achieved by turning in on themselves and engaging in meditative or reflective exercises. For others it means developing relationships with colleagues who allow an open exchange of views and feelings, colleagues who will not be constantly judging our views and challenging our thinking. But at times you will feel uncertain as to how good a guide intuition is really proving to be. You will be suspicious that your own biases and preconceptions are distorting the true picture. These concerns are part of the human condition and it is important to be able to check out the features in the situation that are creating these biases. Asking yourself the following questions will help clarify the sources of these biases. Are you:

- trying to force fit your preconceptions of the solution to the problem?
- allowing strong feelings of like or dislike of a particular individual to cloud your thinking?
- cutting corners in terms of gathering the facts?
- being unnecessarily hasty?
- too tired to be able to enjoy the situation and your role in it?
- more afraid of failing than is usual for you?
- feeling confused and feeling that colleagues are swamping you with their views?
- feeling that your inner voice is not speaking loudly enough to you?

Support networks

People vary enormously in how they use and develop this skill of intuition, but one thing that they have in common is a support network, a means of joining with people who can help them to share feelings and thought processes. In these relationships individuals are prepared to play with their thoughts, allowing arguments to flow and points to be debated even where the outcome is not obviously linked to the issue. This type of interaction is not acceptable in many organizations. Your position, and the organizational climate, may require that you are seen to make key decisions based on hard facts and defensible logic. Many managers find themselves in this position. There are two ways forward here. The first is to use intuition and then present the outcome using logic to frame your decision, supporting it with hard data. The second is to engage in personal development activities that will enhance your intuitive abilities. The checklist below gives some guidance for these activities.

Personal development activities

- Keep a note of situations in which you experience strong feelings that are driven from your intuition. Reflect on these in terms of the outcomes of those that were followed as well as those that were not.

- Practice jotting down thoughts and ideas in the form of mind maps or rich pictures. These show in diagrammatic form how the strategic issues are structured in terms of factors that are changeable and those that are fixed.

- Practice linking the issue or decision to other areas or pursuits in your out-of-work life.

- Read widely and explore the writings of the philosophers and great thinkers of our times.

- Tune into your own thoughts and feelings.

- Value your unconscious mind.

- Practice relaxation techniques and keep physically fit.

- Maintain a tension between your vision and reality.

SUMMARY

You have now completed the two reviews that underpin the skill of mastering the use of intuition. For some individuals anything less than hard-nosed, logically argued and statistically demonstrable decision making smacks of the occult. The reality is that even the most inflexible mind uses intuition. It is just a question of how far that person is prepared to admit, value or expose their thought processes. I have described intuition as the sixth sense that you need to develop as it is the one that is least understood or written about. It is also probably the most difficult to acquire.

Reviewing opportunities for developing multiple and overlapping visions is a very personal but practical activity. The conventional view of creating a vision was seen to be flawed in that not only does the vision change as strategic business games are played out, but a vision, no matter how well thought out and turned into action, has a finite life. There are examples where an original vision has been followed throughout the life of a business. But these are the exceptions and on closer inspection have probably changed in quite fundamental ways. In order to create these evolutionary visions we saw that it was necessary to look beyond the current situation. Our current vision has to be pursued with great vigor and focus, while developing a new but linked vision that will take us into the next era. The challenge is to seek opportunities far beyond our current thinking and this is where we saw the value of engaging in exploratory talks and investing in speculative research and alliances. Seeking to open up the opportunities for creating new visions.

The final review tapped into the ability to harness your imagination as a way of developing intuitive skills. Imagination is voiced through language and metaphor. But in complex situations we saw that imagination underpins the processes used to deal with uncertainty. We have found the need to revisit this question of uncertainty many times in this book. With the intuitive skill we saw that feeling good about a decision meant that we had resolved the uncertainty. At least to a level that gave us the confidence to express our views and commit to action. There are other times when we will feel unsure but still have to force ourselves to make a decision or take action. In a dynamic business environment this is probably the regular diet for many managers. There are ways to check the source of this feeling of uncertainty and learn to identify the areas where this skill needs to be developed. Not the least of these was learning to listen to our inner voices. As a caveat to the more cautious user of this skill we saw that when decisions are made on an intuitive basis it is possible to present them as having been based on logic and rational thought processes.

We have now completed a review of the six generic skills that will enable you to set about bridging the gap between your personal agendas and those of the corporation. With practice you will be able to boast that you have finally made strategy personal. Something that now holds pole position in the race for business and individual success.

Epilogue

The central theme of this book is that every manager can become a better strategist. Better is fine, but becoming one of the best presents two burning challenges. First, how to prepare themselves so that they are able to bring unique plays to the strategy game and dramatically improve their chances of success. Second, discovering how to link personal agendas with those of the organization. In this book I have shown how these twin challenges can be tackled by acquiring a set of generic skills and developing a unique and personal business logic.

The search for a winning business logic, the elusive philosopher's stone, has fuelled the motivation of legions of business managers, strategists, consultants, academics and researchers. Everyone struggles to resolve the enigma that confounds all efforts to anticipate and outsmart their competitor's logic. There is lots of advice on how to compete at an individual level within an organization and on how organizations can compete but very little on how to link the two.

Business, like sport, is only perceived as a game by those who are observing. It has become a spectator sport where the media and writers stand back and comment on how the game is being played and who is doing what to whom and why. The reality for those engaged in the game is that it is a serious and personal struggle to survive, enjoying the odd moment and occasionally reflecting on success. The struggle to make sense of the challenges and opportunities that running and expanding a business presents soon establishes a logic in the mind of the strategist. The shorthand rules and approaches about how to compete become ingrained. A personal logic forms that is used to resolve the complexity of the business situation, make strategic decisions and link strategies and actions to outcomes. The game plays are rehearsed and become familiar friends. Within an industry the game plays are both predictable and easily counteracted. Stalemate for many becomes the only game that can be considered; checkmate is, for most, unthinkable.

Although all strategists have an in-built logic that influences their thinking and actions, it takes more than that to compete successfully in today's dynamic business environment. Businesses prosper and positions of sustainable competitive advantage are created by generating and applying a unique business idea. An idea that explains how resources, within the control of the business, are to be used to create added value for a customer. Initially there may only exist the potential for providing added value but it is this that creates the base from which a business can be built. As businesses develop they spawn multiple business ideas. The inherent danger of this growth process is where a one-time winning business idea continues to be pursued using an inappropriate logic in an inappropriate context. In a successful multi-business the notion that business ideas are born, grow and die is well understood and managed.

So we have the twin pillars of a personal business logic and a business idea establishing the foundations for playing the strategy game. A game that is bedeviled by advice from the crowds pressing from the sidelines. Advice that has been gleaned from watching other games played by other players in other arenas. There is no winning advice and the strategist who wishes to succeed and excel at the game must search for the generic skills that will improve their chances of winning. Skills that will enable a personal logic to be developed and honed so that the game can be approached with a natural confidence and a recognizable style.

The thinking behind this approach can be challenged. It is easy to underestimate the effort required to acquire the six generic skills, particularly those of self development and using intuition. Even more difficult is facing up to the idea of relinquishing approaches which have become old friends. The generic skills have to be understood, valued and then practiced in the hotbed of business competition and organizational life. Not a quest for the fainthearted. But whether we like it or not, these skills are influencing our behavior. If we are already being influenced by them then taking time to reflect on how they are being used and where they are in need of development makes sense. It does require stamina and motivation to do this and for many the payoff will be worth the struggle. The alternative is to become increasingly burdened with approaches that accelerate inefficiencies and reduce the chances of competing in and enjoying business life.

Given the rapid pace of change in business there is a need to go beyond knowledge management and learning how to respond to the new rules and structures created by the information explosion. The game is much too complex to rely for salvation on the latest advice from the gurus or by observing new game plays made by competitors and attempting to follow. We need to go beyond popular debates about core competences, market positioning, relationship marketing, outsourcing, scenario planning and the leveraging of brand strategies. These old frameworks and ways of thinking can be used but must be constantly challenged in order to avoid their becoming established as part of the folklore of business management. The lingua franca of business is important but can shroud the true essence of how the game is being played. The myths quickly cloud the real challenges and issues. Faced with all this complexity and choice the strategist will find that the generic skills remain constant. Without self development, intuition, and having a personal logic that is constantly refreshed, the strategist will not survive, let alone succeed in playing the strategy game and winning.

To become the complete strategist means tackling the strategy game from the mind and not from the rule book. By looking to our inner selves we will be able to create strategies that link our personal agendas with those of the organization. A challenge worth accepting and a voyage worth undertaking.

Index

Adaptation process	181
Adaptor responses	105
Adding value	12, 112
Alexander, Marcus	16
American Express Company	66
Anomalies	82, 188
Argyris, Christopher	126
Asea Brown Boveri	7
AT&T	52, 57
Banc One	17
Ballmer, Steve	58
Barksdale, Jim	57
Benihana	52
Bethlehem Steel	52
Body Shop	63
British Petroleum Amoco	17
Business Idea	28, 59, 109, 116, 122
Business	
Controlling performance in a	169, 173
Drivers of performance in	7
Key issues facing a	120
Measuring performance of a	115, 175
Stakeholders in a	118
Success in	19, 28, 47
Use of language in	80
Business development	
Core competence in	25

Generic strategies in   64, 175
Harnessing dynamic capabilities in   82
Implementation and   117
Logic in   44, 48, 55, 61, 75, 78, 109
Perspectives on   13, 79
Processes in   171, 173, 177
Strategies for   109, 177
Use of dialogue in   134
Use of rhetoric in   135, 141
Business growth
Context and   46, 64, 68, 73, 75, 77, 109
Innovation in   12, 67
Rules for   44, 55
Sources of   12
Trajectories and   73, 125
Business specific effects   46, 50, 55

Cadbury Schweppes   17
Canon   17
Cannion, Rod   30
Campbell, Andrew   16
Capabilities   54, 71
Carnival Corporation   52
Change   72, 188, 199
Chaos   76
Coca-Cola Bottling   52
Cognitive Style   100
Compass   3
Compaq   30
Competitive Advantage   12, 20, 77
Context
Business   46, 64, 68, 73, 77, 109
Changes in   72, 117
Controlling business performance   169
Core competence   25
Courtaulds   17
Creativity   181, 187
Crown Books   54
Culture   26, 143, 146
Cusamano, Michael   57

Decentralization   77
Dell Computers   30

Drucker, Peter   77

Eisner, Michael   29
Emotional response   91
Entrepreneurship   23, 81
Expertise   158

Federal Express   51
Ford, Henry   62
Ford Motor Company   16, 62

Gaining recognition   156
Game playing
    Behavioral theory and   12
    Business as   3
    Competitive groups and   19, 59
    Effects of   79
    Recognition and   156
    Rules of   11
Gannet Corporation   49
General Motors   77
Generic Skill
    Descriptions of   87
    Developing business strategies as a   109
    Developing personal strategies as a   91
    Influencing others as a   131
    Learning how to adapt as a   181
    Taking action in context as a   163
    Using intuition as a   197
Goold, Michael   16
Granada   3

Hamel, Gary   25, 45
Hanson   17
Heijden, Kees   60
Houghton Mifflin   55
Hewlett Packard   70

IBM   30
ICI   17
Imagination   202, 205
Industry development stages   68
Influence   131, 155

Innovation
    Continuous and incremental   67
    Product and process   12
Innovator responses   105
Intuition
    Linking analysis and   133, 206
    Reliance on   197

Kirton, Michael   101
Knowledge
    Explicit and tacit   25, 195
    Using dialogue to create new   134

L.A.Gear   53
Leadership   148
Leadership style audit   152
Learning
    Accelerating   190
    Adaptive and generative   193
    Experience and   123
    Strategy formulation and   24
Language in business   80, 136
Logic
    A universal business   37, 44
    Establishing a business   55, 109
    Finding a winning   61, 75

McDonald's   69
McCaw Cellular   51
McGahan, Anita   49
Mental images held by managers   131, 133
Metaphors used in organizations   131, 144, 195
Microsoft   57
Mintzberg, Henry   21, 76
Mission   96
Models
    Cascading of   111
    Mental   72, 126, 131, 195
    Superior business   48
Multiple frameworks used in organizations   190
Myers–Briggs Type Indicator   100

Nelson Hind   3

Netscape Communications Corporation   57
Nike   53
Nokia   31
Nonaka, I and Takeuchi, H   25

Organization
    Audit of paradoxes used in an   138
    Corporate styles in an   17
    Culture in an   143
    Entrepreneurship in an   81
    Gaining recognition in an   156
    Routines in an   73
    Use of dialogue in an   195
    Use of paradox in an   80
Ollila, Jorma   31

Paradoxes
    Auditing organizational   138
    Balancing   73, 142
    Organizational   57, 136
Parenting style   17
Performance in business   115, 175
Personal strategies
    Developing   91
    Vision and   95
    Goals and   96
    Mission statements and   99
    Roles and   99
Personality
    Cognitive style and   100
    Traits and   101
Perspectives on business development 13, 21, 79
Peters, Thomas   78
Pfeiffer, Echard   30
PIMS   46
Politics   26, 135
Porter, Michael   23
Power   26, 135, 176
Prahalad, C.K.   25, 45

Quinn, James   24

Rhetoric   135

Rules for success   44, 55

Schumpeter, Joseph   81
Self-worth   93
Shareholders   167
Sloan, Alfred   15
Sodexho Gardner Merchant   3
Sony Corporation   65, 69
Sprint-Fon Group   54
Stakeholders
    Analysis of   118, 164
    Balancing the   163, 168
    Pressure from   167
Starbucks   51
Stockholders   56, 61
Strategy formation
    Cognition in   24
    Configuration in   27
    Culture in   26
    Design as   21
    Entrepreneurs in   23
    Environment in   26
    Intent in   45
    Learning as   24
    Planning as   21, 57, 76
    Positioning in   23, 79
    Power and politics in   26
    Use of models in   109
Strategies
    Assumptions behind   132
    Characteristics of successful   28, 177
    Contextualized   64, 71
    Cost leadership   66
    Declining industry   70
    Developing business   109
    Differentiation   65
    Effective   177
    Embryonic and growth industry   69
    First mover   69
    Generic   64, 175
    Implementation of   68, 117
    Intent of   45
    Market focus   67

Mature industry 69
Mix of generic 68
Personal 91
Positioning 20, 23, 79
Product differentiation 65
Resource based 20, 25, 79
Trajectory effects on 72
Vertical integration 70
Winning 71, 177
Strategic thinking
   Impact of language on 80
   Planning and 61, 76

Trajectories in business 72, 125
Turner Broadcasting 54

Venturing 25, 199
Vision building 95, 197, 200

Walt Disney 28
Whittington, R. 14
Whole Earth Company 37
Winning strategies 71, 177

Yoffie, David 57